Parenting, SportsMom Style

Real-Life Solutions for Surviving the Youth Sports Scene

Laurel Phillips and Barbara Stahl

307 Books

MAUMEE, OHIO

Parenting, SportsMom Style:
Real-Life Solutions for Surviving the Youth Sports Scene

© 2000 by Laurel Phillips and Barbara Stahl

ISBN 0-9659445-5-7

Cover illustration by Becky Aubry
SportsMom™ comics by Kevin Ewing, Ewing Illustration and
  Robin Williamson, Robin Williamson Illustration & Design
Interior illustrations by Becky Aubry and Kevin Ewing
Interior and cover production by Troy Scott Parker, Cimarron Design

SportsMom™ is a registered trademark of KBL

Published by 307 Books
P.O. Box 993
Maumee, OH 43537
phone: 1-888-307-2046
fax: 419-893-5737
e-mail: bstahl307@aol.com

The Good Stuff Inside

Acknowledgments

A SIMPLE, SINCERE **THANK YOU** to all of our personal friends for their encouragement, and to all of our professional friends for their help and their generous contributions. We'd also like to acknowledge those moms and acquaintances who helped to fill in the gaps with specifics about the sports with which we have no personal experience.

We extend fervent recognition to our editor, Barb Meyer, an integral member of the SportsMom team. Barb brought much more to the project than just her clever wordsmithing, personal examples, and keen sense of humor; believe us when we say we could not have done this without her.

We're grateful to Laurel's husband, David, and to Barbara's collective family for their love and support. And we lovingly identify our children—Teka, Elizabeth, Morgan, Pete, and Ben—as our source of inspiration. Each moment we have shared in their sports endeavors—the laughs and excitement, the disappointments and angst—is a precious memory. We're not quite sure who's learned more from the experiences, the kids or us. But we know as we watch them becoming wonderful young adults that every 5:30 a.m. alarm and every mile on the road have been worth it. It's a long way from being over: we plan to stay buckled up.

Introduction

IN 1998, WE PUBLISHED our first book, *SOS! Soccer On the Sidelines: A Guide to Competitive Travel Soccer for Serious Soccer Moms.* Based on our own experience as once-novice travel soccer moms, we were reasonably certain that there was an audience for *SOS!,* but even we were surprised at just how well the book was received. We got calls from all over the country, and enjoyed favorable write-ups in national publications such as *Sports Illustrated for Kids' SportsParents* and *USA Weekend,* and the *Los Angeles Times.*

However, we were absolutely amazed by how the issues we presented rang true for such a wide variety of moms and sports: each and every one saw herself in the soccer book and said "that's *my* life!" We quickly realized that a new soccer mom isn't the only parent totally unprepared for what lies ahead the day her child decides he wants to get involved in a sport.

And so we decided to write *Parenting, SportsMom Style: Real-Life Solutions for Surviving the Youth Sports Scene.* We've done our best in this book to cover everything a mom handling her role as SportsMom needs to know—from the big philosophical issues to the small everyday details that can drive you nuts.

If you're just starting out as the mom of a child in sports, this book can provide you with valuable information to help you better plan your journey. If you're already on the SportsMom trail—and find yourself stumbling in the dark upon occasion—we hope *Parenting, SportsMom Style* shines a little light on your path.

aka Laurel Phillips and Barbara Stahl

Please Note: As you read this book you'll notice we used masculine pronouns. This is a grammatical—not political— statement.

PART ONE

Welcome to the World of SportsMom

SportsMom™

© 1998 KBL

"Mom, is it OK if Julie throws up in our new van?"

Chapter 1

What Have You Gotten Yourself Into? (and What Are You Going to Do Now That You're Here?)

IT BEGINS INNOCENTLY ENOUGH. Your child rushes home one day to announce, "Mom, I want to play *fill in name of sport here!*"

"A few practices, a few games, a few bucks for a uniform," you say to yourself. "No big deal."

If you're like most Rookie SportsMoms, that's precisely what you think—right up till the day it finally dawns on you that it *is* a big deal. It doesn't matter which sport or level of play your child finally got involved in: it's playing havoc with your schedule, your checkbook, and the mileage limit on your minivan lease. Once this reality sinks in, you have two choices: to ignore it, or deal with it.

If you ignore it, you'll be passing up two important opportunities. First, you'll lose the opportunity to manage the sport, rather than letting it control you. Second, you'll sacrifice the opportunity to use your child's sport as the terrific parenting vehicle it can be.

Using youth sports as a means to shape your child's character, his values, and his relationship with you, your family, and others is the very essence of being a SportsMom. It's taking the potential of a relatively new phenomenon in our culture—organized youth sports—and maximizing it for the benefit of your child and your family.

Boldly Going Where Few Moms Have Gone Before

About now, you may be saying to yourself, "Hey, all this sounds great in theory, but the world of organized youth sports is new to me. How do I handle this SportsMom gig—maximizing potential, taking advantage of opportunities, bleaching sweatsocks—when I know nothing about the way this world works, and have no idea what I'm getting involved in?"

Relax, SportsMom, because you're not alone.

Relax, SportsMom, because you're not alone. Organized sports are unknown territory to most moms. When we grew up, organized sports were pretty much limited to seasonal high school teams or Little League® play.

However, somewhere, somehow, sometime on the way to the Nineties, massive numbers of kids found their way into organized sports. As we write this book, an estimated forty-five million American youngsters between the ages of six and eighteen are enrolled in some type of organized sport, in levels of play that range from recreational teams to the Olympic Development Program.

Why the explosion in youth sports in the past two decades? We're not sociologists; however, we'll give it a shot.

In our opinion, the growth of organized youth sports has its roots in major societal change in the last half of the Twentieth Century. In the Fifties, Sixties, and early Seventies, Americans satisfied their innate desire for community through the geographic neighborhoods in which they lived. Stay-at-home moms were the stuff of which the neighborhood community was made, the fibers that held it together. These moms performed a function vital to all communities: by virtue of their presence in the neighborhood, they nurtured and protected the young.

However, as more and more moms started working outside the home, they had little time to interact. The tapestry of neighborhood community unraveled, and, for a while, nothing arose to take its place. We regretted its passing, and longed for the role it played, not only in protecting our children, but also in making our own lives fuller and richer. However, we were too busy trying to work, get supper on the table, and find adequate child care to figure out a way to replace it.

Fortunately, a series of events was taking place that eventually resulted in filling that vacuum:

- Sports coverage on television steadily increased, in the process exposing us to a variety of sports besides football and baseball.

- Title IX became law in 1972, requiring schools to spend equal amounts of money on girls' sports. Suddenly, we were confronted with a new concept: It's okay for girls—not just the tomboys—to play sports, too.
- As a society, we began to recognize the danger of allowing kids to interact in the neighborhood without a lot of moms at home. Kids with nothing to do and no supervision tended to get in trouble, and trouble in the late Seventies and Eighties wasn't limited to filching flowers from the neighbor's garden or toilet-papering houses: trouble could mean pre-teen sex, alcohol, drugs, and gangs.

Together, those factors resulted in kids' becoming more and more involved in organized sports. Today, organized sports help do what the neighborhood community once did.

They facilitate social interaction among children, adults, and families. Sports also provide an opportunity for shared responsibilities, like carpooling, or watching out for another SportsMom's kid when she's too sick to make the competition.

Above all, organized sports are a safe place for kids to be.

And so, as we see it, organized sports grew to help fill the gap left by the demise of the neighborhood community. This has resulted in less unstructured family time, and more time spent fulfilling obligations to your child's sport. It's why you, SportsMom, cart your kids to practices, games, and competitions year-round, when a generation ago, such activity was relatively rare, or at least pretty much seasonal.

Now, as we move into the future, organized sports are taking on another role. In a world in which communication is increasingly impersonal—think *voice mail, fax,* and *e-mail—*

SportsMom™

"It's part of their persona."

organized sports require personal, face-to-face contact. They fill the need—our kids' and our own—to connect with real live human beings outside of school and work.

We're sharing all this theoretical stuff because we think it's important to understand precisely what organized sports represent in our society, and the opportunities they present. That team isn't simply a team: it's your family's new neighborhood. The other athletes, parents, and coaches are your neighbors. This is a safe place where you've chosen to raise your child. It looks different than the old neighborhood you probably grew up in, but it has the potential to function just the same—if you recognize and make the most of it.

But doing that can be difficult, because your new neighborhood is woefully short on tour guides. No one from the Organized Sports Welcome Wagon arrives on your doorstep to tell you the local customs. Even your own mother is not much help because—unless you were an Olympic athlete—she never lived in the Neighborhood of Organized Youth Sports.

A Guide to Your New Neighborhood

However, there is help on the horizon, because we've been where you're sitting right now. We've faced the same challenges, big and little. And, in the process of meeting them, we've charted our way through the unfamiliar neighborhood of organized sports.

Between the two of us, we have twenty-three years of experience as SportsMoms to five children (two girls and three boys) who have participated in seven different sports at a variety of levels of play. One of us is a Married SportsMom; the other, the Single Variety. At times, we've handled our role with style and grace. On other occasions, we've stumbled our way through and made colossal mistakes.

However, good or bad, these experiences taught us a lot, and—since we lived to tell the tale—we want to share what we've learned with you. That's why we wrote this book, a combination map/survival guide to organized youth sports from a SportsMom point of view. It's designed to shorten your SportsMom learning curve and help you make the entire experience a better one for your player, your family, and you.

Chapter 2

Ask What Sports Can Do for Your Child— and What You Must Do for Your Child's Sport

THE MOST IMPORTANT THING you can do as a SportsMom is to recognize the potential of organized sports to help your child and your family develop in positive ways.

First, let's take a look at what youth sports can do for your child.

Sports can teach your child Important Lessons of Life. In fact, you name the Life Lesson, and there's a very good chance the sports experience can teach it: how to set and achieve a personal goal; the satisfaction of mastering skills; the importance and how-to's of working with others; the joy and camaraderie of being part of something larger than oneself.

Yes, all these and more are covered in the Organized Sports' Life Lesson Plan.

Interacting with Coach teaches your child Important Life Lessons on grappling with, and respecting, the rules and authority of someone besides you. Sports can teach your child how to handle both disappointment and triumph. They can help him appreciate and respect that there are others who are better at something than he is, and still others who must struggle to achieve what comes easily to him. They can improve his ability to communicate and help him mature.

Youth sports can help your kid build a strong body, and instill good fitness habits at an early age. They provide him with a positive outlet for his energy. They may keep him out of trouble. Youth sports also give him a chance to belong and have fun. And, above all, they can help build his self-esteem and character.

Now, what can sports do for your family?

When your child chooses to participate in a sport, your family is forced to spend lots of time together. You're what we call "car-captive." You share experiences and make memories with one another. You have plenty of time to talk, without the distraction of television or the computer. You observe more about your child—what's important to him, what he's thinking about, the things that worry him—as you travel to practice after practice, competition after competition. At the same time, by listening to what you say and watching what you do, he picks up on your values. All that time together provides you with opportunities to relate your child's sports experiences to real life so those Important Lessons hit home.

So how is this different than the rest of your life? After all, you may already spend time together and log plenty of miles on the minivan.

There are two major differences.

Once your child hits middle school (age eleven or twelve), his peers and other activities start to look a lot more appealing to him than you do: the result is less time spent with good old Mom and Dad. That means you don't have the chance to stay as connected as you were before—unless youth sports continue to provide you with the opportunity to spend lots of time together, sharing common experiences. When you spend the amount of time with your child that youth sports necessitate, you can't *not* know what's going on in his life.

And that brings us to the second difference. When you and your child spend time together because of his sport, you are connecting in an activity he *wants* to do.

Think about it: how much of your child's life does he actually have control over? The government decides he should go to school. You decide the house rules. He may make more choices as he grows older, but, by and large, you make most of his big decisions for him, or establish fairly tight guidelines for his choices. And that is how it should be. After all, you are the parent, and he is not. However, it's the reason your child sometimes enters family-planned activities with little enthusiasm.

Sports, however, is a different story. He is excited about participating, and willing to cooperate in order to ensure your cooperation and participation. Most SportsMoms will tell you that the issue of choice makes all the difference in the world in kids' attitudes—at least most of the time.

What Your Journey Requires

We've established that youth sports, by their very nature, can do many good things for your child and your family. Those things won't happen, however, if you and your child do not make commitments to seeing this endeavor through.

If you're not sure what the game will require of your child, call a Veteran SportsMom on his prospective team, or the appropriate sports league, club, association, or recreation department. Then think through any requirements you want to add, such as keeping up his grades, or picking up extra household chores to free you to pilot the station wagon. Make sure your list is complete, then go over it with your child before the season starts.

He must agree—up front, while he's still riding high on a wave of enthusiasm—to follow through on the actual requirements of his sport. As SportsMom, you need to make sure he knows what he's agreeing to: showing up at practices, working out at home, staying with the team for the duration of the commitment he makes, and so on. Following through on his commitment also means fulfilling your added requirements.

Your child must understand this is a tit-for-tat, *quid-pro-quo*, I'll-scratch-your-back-if-you'll-scratch-mine kind of deal (adjusted for age, of course). He wants to play sports, *ergo* he must do what is required to play. That in itself is one of Life's Most Important Lessons.

Don't throw the "expectation" list away: pull it out someday when he doesn't want to do those extra chores he agreed to. (We assure you: like death and taxes, that day will come.) Remind him that *he* agreed of his own free will, and, based

SportsMom™

"What do you mean, 'I'm too sick to go to practice this morning?'"

upon his agreement, *you* agreed to drive him to practices. (You'll no doubt hear the gears in his brain clicking as he puts those two thoughts together and comes to the startling realization that he risks his ride when he doesn't keep up his end of the deal.)

Of course, as SportsMom, your commitment means more than dropping your kid off at practice. Using sports as an effective parenting vehicle requires *being there* and *being aware.*

At the most basic level, *being there* means just that: showing up every time it counts. That doesn't just mean for games. It means for practices, for fund-raisers, for group meetings. If you're not prepared to do those things, you're doing your child a grave disservice: in the case of practices, for instance, your unwillingness to be on time every time can result in his losing game playing time, or if he's in an individual sport, losing valuable coaching time. On a more personal level, you're also telling him that what matters so very much to him doesn't matter very much to you. So, if you want to do this SportsMom thing right, you must make a commitment to be present and accounted for when it matters.

> More than anything else— more than making the team, more than friends, more than a trip to Disney World— your kid wants your time and your attention.

(There are times, of course, when you cannot be physically present. Serious illness and Acts of God are considered pretty good reasons, and certain allowances are made for single parents or parents with several kids playing different sports at the same time. Even in those cases, though, the onus is on you to make certain your child gets where he needs to be when he needs to be there.)

So we've established that you must *be there* as much as you possibly can. However, *being there* doesn't just mean your physical presence. It also means expressing interest in something your child wants to do. More than anything else—more than making the team, more than friends, more than a trip to Disney World—your kid wants your time and your attention. There's no better way to give him those things than by becoming involved in his sports life, this activity *he* has exercised his free will to take part in.

Being aware means staying alert to opportunities the sports experience presents to teach your child the Important Lessons of Life we've already mentioned in this chapter. Those lessons aren't always obvious to your child. Sometimes it takes a little prompting from you for him to comprehend those lessons; sometimes you have to act with all the subtlety of a Mack truck to get them through his head.

Bottom line, it's your responsibility to guide your child through his sports experience. You must recognize that while leagues can organize and coaches can instruct and managers can schedule, no one but you can help your kid get as much as possible out of the time he spends involved in his sport.

As Veteran SportsMoms, we'd be lying if we said this is always an easy job. But we can say with certainty that it's an important job, and one worth doing well.

SportsMom™

HUM-
WHIRR...

© 1998 KBL

"I always thought 'Zamboni'® was a kind of ice cream..."

C h a p t e r   3

Know Thy Sport

As SportsMom, sometimes you have input into your child's decision to play a particular sport. Sometimes, your child already knows what he wants to play. Other times, by virtue of geography or culture, your child's choice of sport is no choice at all: there's one sport to choose from in your hometown of East Snake Navel, USA, and he either plays it or he doesn't.

No matter which of these three scenarios you face, *what* you want a sport to do for *your* child is always *your* decision. If you can steer your kid toward a sport that is ideal for helping you accomplish your goals, terrific. If the choice of sport has already been made for you, you still have the power to frame your child's experience in a way that benefits him.

Remember in Chapter 1 when we said that organized youth sports is your new neighborhood?

Well, if you get to choose your child's sport, it's like deciding exactly which house you're going to buy in that neighborhood. You're looking for one that's going to meet

the needs of your child and your family, doesn't require more time for upkeep than you can give it, and won't break the family budget. If your child has already chosen his sport (or if there is no choice but one where you live), it's more like being transferred to your new neighborhood to live in a house of your employer's choosing. In that case, your job is to make the house fit your needs, your time, and your budget.

However, whichever situation you're in, if you're going to make your child's sport work for you and your family, you must understand the nature of that sport. That's what this chapter is designed to help you do.

Of course, it's impossible for us to examine each of the vast number of youth sports individually, unless we want to get into a serious competition with *War and Peace* for shelf space in the local bookstore. Instead, we'll take a look at sports in a general way, pointing out the issues you need to take into consideration as you frame your strategy for using sports as a tool to help your child grow, develop, and learn Important Lessons of Life.

Individual vs. Team Sports

The most useful place for us to start is the issue of individual versus team sports. Any Veteran SportsMom will tell you that these are two distinct experiences, both of which can teach your child good things. Let's take a look at a few of the characteristics of individual and team sports:

Individual Sport	Team Sport
Focuses on developing individual skills	*Focuses on developing teamwork*
Stresses individual responsibility	*Stresses responsibility to the group*
Primary interaction with an adult coach	*Interaction with adult coach and fellow players*
Spotlight on individual performance	*Focus on team performance*

If you have the option of helping your child choose a sport, the direction in which you guide him—individual or team—is going to depend upon what you are trying to accomplish through this experience.

If you've got a loner who desperately needs a group experience, you may want to nudge him in the direction of a team sport. On the other hand, a natural loner who has athletic talent may have what it takes to excel in an individual sport, such as figure skating. If your child lacks strong male role models in his life, an individual sport has the potential to provide him with a great deal of interaction with a male coach you consider to be a positive influence.

In selecting a sport, you should also take into consideration the amount of pressure your child can handle. Perhaps he needs an individual sports experience to help him learn to better manage pressure; maybe he needs to escape into the anonymity of a team until he's better prepared to deal with it. On the other hand, if he's hesitant to try a sport because he lacks natural athletic ability, an individual sport may be the right place for him to receive the extra support and coaching he needs to overcome his eye-hand-body coordination problems.

You should be aware that many sports we generally think of as individual—swimming, ice skating, gymnastics, archery, golf—impose team scoring at the youth level to create a team concept. In fact, in some of these sports, like ice skating, kids start out learning as a group, or club, eventually work their way up to individual coaching, but still remain part of the club. Olympian Tara Lipinski, for example, remained loyal to her skating club right up through her gold medal performance. This individual sport/team concept can give young athletes who want to pursue an individual sport the opportunity to experience group dynamics.

As you contemplate all these factors, remember that you know your child better than anyone, including your child himself. We can't tell you what your child should get from his sports experience, but we can tell you that it's a wise SportsMom who looks at the big picture of what a sport offers, then draws her battle plan.

You need a battle plan *if* you have a say in the sport your child selects. You need an even better battle plan *if you don't* have a say: for example, if you hoped he'd choose an individual sport to strengthen his sense of personal responsibility, how are you going to use the team sport he's chosen to do the same thing? It's a bit harder, but rest assured, there's no challenge too great for that extraordinary creature known as SportsMom.

You also need a battle plan—General Schwartzkopf quality—for a situation we touched on earlier: when your child's choice is no choice. You may live in an area of the country where there's one sport—and your kid stinks at it. You may be in a town where the prevailing philosophy is that "real men" play football and only "sissies" play soccer. Or, your child may want to play a specific sport, but none of the people who coach it in your area are particularly good role models, or no one coaches it at all.

In cases like these, you need to employ all your SportsMom skills to do what's best for your child. Always remember that it's not so much the reality of the situation that is going to affect your kid, but how you help him interpret and frame that reality. In the instance of the less-than-perfect coach, for example, you can teach your child that it is possible to respect a person's authority while disagreeing with things he does or says.

Over the years, we've discovered that these less-than-ideal situations provide better opportunities to teach a child to deal with real life than do those situations in which all the elements are positive. Learning to deal with that flawed coach today can prepare your child to deal with an unreasonable boss in the future.

Personally, we've both encouraged our kids to take part, at different times in their lives, in both individual and team sports. We wanted them to experience the group dynamics of being on a team, but we also wanted them to become involved in individual sports because people tend to continue to pursue them as adults. After all, it's a whole lot simpler to find a tennis partner at age thirty-five than it is to find twenty-one other guys for a football game.

We also made it clear to all our children that not participating in sports was simply not an option. We wanted them to incorporate regular, fun, physical activity into their lives at an early age, so early, in fact, that they would never consider exercise and fitness optional.

Time and Money

Let's move on now to some of the more practical factors you need to think about as your child becomes involved in sports.

First, you need to find out what kind of time this sport will demand of you and your child.

To do that, talk to as many Veteran SportsMoms as you can find. Remember: it's not just practice and game time you need to know about. It's travel time, fund-raising time, extra laundry time, team meeting time, and time spent at home developing skills, all multiplied by the length of the season, from the first pre-season activity to the last post-season tournament buzzer. If you and your child aren't prepared to put in the time, don't sign up for the sport. That's a much better Life Lesson for him to learn than signing up, then not fulfilling your commitment.

Second, find out what this sport is going to cost. Again, consult experienced SportsMoms. Ask about playing fees, the cost of equipment, and facility or field rental times, *e.g.,* ice time. Are tournaments on the schedule, and, if so, how much out-of-town, overnight travel is involved—and what does it cost? Find out if Coach is paid or volunteers his time. See if extra personal coaching is the norm among athletes: if so, what does that cost? Ask where costs can be cut without compromising the quality of your child's play or endangering his safety (used equipment). And don't forget about the incidentals that add up: gas, take-out meals you wouldn't buy otherwise, end-of-season gifts for Coach, and after-game treats.

Generally, when it comes to time and money, individual sports require more than team sports, and higher levels of play, like travel teams, require more than sports played at the recreational level. A good rule of thumb is that no matter how much time and money you think your kid's sport will take, it will take more. That brings us to our next point.

We recognize that organized youth sports can put a strain on some families' budgets. If money is a problem, don't be afraid to ask the club or other organizing body about scholarships. Many groups set aside funds just to make certain kids who want to play can. If club scholarship funds aren't available where you live, explore other options, like teams organized by the YMCA, YWCA, the Boys and Girls Club, and neighborhood centers: many receive United Way or other charitable funding specifically to cover the expenses of children who can't afford them. School teams may also be less expensive, and prepared to help with fees and uniform costs.

Don't let your pride stand in the way of asking for help, and don't be afraid your child will be treated differently because he's receiving financial aid. It's been our experience that the only way the other kids know he's receiving assistance is if he tells them.

One final point about money and youth sports: if your child's current sport fits into the family budget, but the second sport he wants to play won't, we think it's perfectly okay to be up front with him about the situation. One of Life's Lessons is that we don't always have enough money to do everything we'd like. This is a good time to help your child accept that reality, and learn how to make choices based on it: *Which sport does he want more? If he's older, could he earn enough money doing odd jobs or mowing lawns to pay for his second sport (without jeopardizing his grades, of course)? Is he willing to do the "legwork" of investigating financial aid possibilities?*

If you explore all those options together, and the bottom line is that he can play just one sport, you'll probably feel bad, but don't feel guilty. By helping him face financial reality, you've begun to prepare him for situations he'll face many times in the future. If, on the other hand, you shelter him from that reality and require the family to make major sacrifices to finance his second sport, you may be setting your child up to believe he's entitled to what he wants, no matter the cost to others. When you look at it that way, SportsMom, making him face financial reality is good, not bad.

Multiple Sports

Having touched on the financial strain multiple sports can place on you and your family, we'd now like to discuss the strain they put on your schedule.

The issue of more than one sport often comes later in the process. But, like life, chapters don't always flow in apple pie order, and this seems as good a time as any to address multiple sports. So here goes.

When kids are very young, just beginning their sports experience, some SportsMoms believe they should provide their kids the opportunity to take part in a variety of sports. We think that's reasonable at that point in their lives: sports are usually less expensive and time-consuming at that level;

your child enjoys a lot of different activities but is committed to no one in particular; and you, Eager Young SportsMom that you are, have plenty of energy.

However, there will come a time—usually when your child is eleven or twelve— when that philosophy may no longer be smart thinking. He's at a higher level of play now, and that means more money and more time. Even if you have the money to handle multiple sports, the increased time and energy required remains an issue.

True, you can buy time. But take it from two SportsMoms who have done their level best to purchase as much time as possible: unless you're independently wealthy, you can't buy enough to make a significant dent in an overburdened schedule.

If you and your child believe he can handle two sports with separate seasons, or you think you can straddle two sports that overlap for a month or so, that's one thing. If your child is in two sports with identical seasons, that is quite another, particularly if you have other kids who play yet other sports at the same time. Then you're facing significant time-crunch issues that affect your athlete, your family, Coach, teammates and their parents, and you.

Let's start with Coach, teammates, and their parents. If your child is juggling two sports that overlap to any degree, chances are he'll be missing practices in one sport to make them in another. He may even need to decide between two competitions that fall on the same day. If he's on a team, his fellow athletes will become irritated at having to accommodate those absences, and their parents will tire of overlooking the number of practices your kid is allowed to miss and still play. Coach will end up in an awkward situation. No one will win, especially your child.

Multiple sports can also demand too much of your athlete, your family, and you—even if they don't overlap. We are firm believers that children need unscheduled time just to be kids: always having a sport going on may mean they don't get it. Your family needs that same kind of down time, and you do, too. There are those who disagree with the last part of that statement, but we've found they're the same folks who spell *mother* M-A-R-T-Y-R.

It's your job to know when your child, your family, and you are pushing beyond your capacity, when you're handling too much, too often, and for too long. It's your responsibility to make sure that rearing your young athlete does not turn into a family marathon. You want your kids to look back someday and remember plenty of fun times hanging out together as a family, not just endless hours spent traveling to practices in a minivan piloted by a SportsMom in emotional overdrive.

Talent and Skill

Another area you should think about in choosing/using your child's sport is the level at which he hopes to play.

Organized youth sports offers levels of involvement that range from rec teams with once-a-week practices and games for a six-week season to Olympic Development Programs with twice-a-day practices and intense competitions year-round. Depending upon his skill, your child can participate at the rec level, a school level, a club level, a travel level, a tournament level, or regional or national level.

The level at which your child ends up playing most often depends on his talent and the effort he puts forth to develop it. But when you're just starting out on this sports venture, you don't know where he's at, talent or commitment-wise. The best thing you and your child can do is pick a sport and a level you're comfortable with, and see what happens. Later on, you can help your child take an objective look at his talent to determine if he needs to adjust his level of play up or down. Remember: while you want a level of play to present your child with challenges, you don't want it to be so far beyond his abilities that he finds the entire experience frustrating or humiliating.

As long as we're on the subject of talent and skill, we want to focus briefly on handling situations where not all brothers and sisters are created equal. This is a tough one, SportsMom. You're proud of your Super Athlete and don't want to overlook his accomplishments, but in the process you don't want to crush the spirit of your Delightful But Definite Klutz. Often the differential isn't that extreme, but the issue is essentially the same.

So what do you do? We suggest you don't ignore individual accomplishments, but that you make certain your child realizes that athletic accomplishment is not the only kind you value. *Every* child is good at something. Your job is to praise your children for all their accomplishments, not just the sports' variety. However, we add this warning: never place a greater value on accomplishment than you do on good character. As SportsMom, your primary goal is raising a decent human being; if he also turns out to be a decent athlete, that's great, but secondary.

In addition to focusing on each child's individual accomplishments, try to steer your kids clear of competing in the same arena. Being in different sports or activities can lessen the obvious differences in skill levels. However, if you have a less-talented child who insists on following in his hyper-talented sibling's footsteps, make sure he understands what he's getting into. Help him set his own goals for the sport, instead of replicating his brother or sister's.

If you discover that his only goal is to beat his sibling because he wants to gain status in the family, you'd better take a good hard look at the signals you've been sending your kids. Do you focus more time, attention, praise, or resources on the talented one? If so, you need to change your attitude and actions; apologies may even be in order. If you honestly examine your behavior and it's not out of line, then you need to discover why your less-talented child feels he must excel to gain your favor. Sometimes it's because he's totally misinterpreted something you said or did. Sometimes it's his own expectations or wrong thinking causing the problem. Whatever the reason, you've got to make sure he understands that you value him for who he is, not for what he does.

How Young is Too Young?

Another factor in choosing a sport is the age of your child. Today, kids as young as five are routinely involved in organized sports. That's okay with us, as long as we use the term *organized* loosely.

We think it's great to see little kids playing tee-ball, or skating their hearts out in hopes of becoming the next Michelle Kwan. We even think belonging to a team and going to practices can be good for kids this age—if the right coach is involved. Kids this age need a coach who can find  the fun in watching, for example, a group of tiny soccer players all packed together, following the ball, even though the team just finished a passing drill.

However, we don't hold with the view that children should become involved in serious, competitive sports very early in their little lives to give them a leg up later.

Very young children do not have fully-developed muscles and bones: they can't handle the physical demands of serious training. At age six or seven, children have yet to develop the head-to-body proportion that comes later in childhood: their heads are now huge in relation to the size of their torsos, legs, and arms. And the minds contained in those "big" heads aren't prepared to handle the rigors of training, either.

If you're still tempted to enroll your tiny player in a competitive sport, remember this: the exceptional athlete is just that—exceptional, and often born with qualities that predispose him to excel. One of us once saw a picture of Olympic Gold Medal Decathlete Bruce Jenner as a toddler. He already looked like he'd been pumping iron: broad shoulders, muscular chest, narrow waist, no baby fat anywhere. Since he probably wasn't getting steroids in his pablum, it's safe to assume he was born that way.

Everyone who starts early in a sport does not translate that early start into success. If your child wants to get involved in a sport at an early age, we'd encourage you to emphasize the fun of playing, the enjoyment of the game, the pleasure of running, skipping, and throwing. After all, childhood goes by so fast that it doesn't hurt to let them linger there for a while.

Being on a Winning Team: Is It Important?

If you're like most SportsMoms, when your child starts out in a sport, your primary worry is that he'll make the team— any team. You don't want him to experience the sting of rejection; as long as he makes it somewhere, you're happy.

However, as time goes on, most SportsMoms want their child to be on, if not a winning team, at least one of the top teams in that sport in their community.

It's easy to understand why SportsMom wants that. If her child is winning, he'll have more fun and feel better about himself: it's automatic, it's easy, and it doesn't add to the Great SportsMom Burden of framing the sports experience to achieve good things in her child's life.

However, the reality is that if one team wins, another loses, so not every SportsMom can get her wish. And, even if your child ends up on last year's championship team, there's no guarantee that team will win a single game this season.

SportsMom™

"Shake it off! Shake it off!!"

So what's a SportsMom to do? We suggest that you look not so much at a team's win/lose record as at its coach's philosophy on winning and losing. Does it match yours?

We're not going to tell you what that philosophy ought to be: that's up to you. You know how much pressure your child can take. You know the values you want to instill in him. Just make sure that what he learns from Coach will teach him the Life Lessons on Winning and Losing *you* want him to learn.

Now, having said all that, let us say this: we know you realize, intellectually, that your child may not always be able to win, that he may even learn greater lessons from losing, and so forth and so on. However, inside the breast of all True SportsMoms is an inextinguishable ember of emotion that flickers to the mantra, "I want my kid to win. I want my kid to win. I want my kid to win."

Of course you do. We do, too. And do you know why? Because when our kids lose, it reflects on us—or at least we *think* it does. As in a vision, we suddenly see all the years of our child's life stretching ahead of him, filled with welfare checks and broken relationships and a Greek chorus of bystanders chanting, "You must have had a real screw-up for a mother."

We mention this because we want you to know that the disconnect you feel between your intellect ("Of course my child must lose sometimes.") and your emotions ("He's gotta win!") comes with the SportsMom territory. Every other Veteran SportsMom standing on the sidelines or sitting in the stands is feeling that same disconnect. The key is not to let your emotions overcome that veneer of civilized intellect you've got in place: expecting your child to always win puts too much pressure on him.

So get a grip, SportsMom, and commit that old chestnut to heart: *It's not whether you win or lose but how you play the game.* Repeat as needed—and trust us, it will be.

It's His Childhood

We've already said that it's fair to ask your child to base his choice of sport on practical factors, such as the amount of time you have available or the money you can afford to spend. (We've both had to ask our kids to pass on additional sports for these reasons.)

However, we don't think it's fair to encourage your child to choose a sport based on *your* emotional needs. Your child's sports experience is not intended as a place for you to relive your glory days as an athlete, or even to vicariously experience sports participation you may have missed as a child.

The purpose of your child's sports experience is to provide him and your family with opportunities to grow and develop. Your role in his sports experience is to maximize and facilitate those opportunities, not to live through your child.

About now you may be saying to yourself, "Of course I'm not going to be one of *those* parents. I won't rant at Coach because he doesn't put my kid in the game. I won't get upset and scream at the ref when I don't like a call. I'm not about to yell at my child because he didn't push harder or accuse him of acting like a baby if he cries at a loss. And I certainly won't insist he take up the sport I (choose one) loved in high school *or* always wanted to play but couldn't."

That's good. But living through your child isn't always as obvious as that. In fact, it can be as subtle as paying more attention to what he's doing in his sport than how he's feeling about it, or more grandly celebrating his successes in sport than in other areas of his life. It can manifest itself in your being more nervous about an upcoming competition than your child is. It can even show up as anger if he wants to switch sports or quit them altogether.

It's really easy to fall into this behavior. Any parent who has lived through her child's first piano recital or at-bat knows the sweaty-palmed, heart-pounding fear that goes with that territory. That's normal. But when it continues or intensifies to the point that you have trouble finding the joy in simply watching your child perform, be very, very careful.

You've taken your first step on the slippery path to the Land of Overbearing SportsMoms.

Chances are, your good common sense will give you a tweak to let you know you're headed in the wrong direction, and when it does, do your child and yourself a favor and pay attention. Don't let a healthy parental interest in your child's sport turn ugly by entwining your own sense of self with your child's. Always remember that this is *his* childhood, *his* sport, and *his* life.

What About the Future?

We don't think there's a young athlete alive who hasn't imagined batting in the winning run in the World Series, capturing the Olympic Gold in figure skating, being the next Tiger Woods, or <u>fill in the sports fantasy here</u>. If her child shows talent as he advances in his sport, it's a Rare SportsMom who doesn't occasionally indulge in those fantasies, too.

Fantasies aside, where might your child's sport take him in terms of educational and career opportunities? And why is it important to ask that question so early in his sports experience? Let's address the second question first.

Although your child may just be starting his sports experience, we think it's wise to give at least some thought to the role sports will play in his future—mainly to make sure you don't overestimate it. Yes, it's fun to indulge in fantasies about his scoring a touchdown during a sudden death playoff in the Super Bowl. But it's unwise, no matter how talented your child, to assume that his ability will translate into a college, Olympic, or professional career. There are parents and children who do, and, unfortunately, many of them don't have backup plans in place in case sports don't pan out.

We think it's wiser to be realistic about where sports might take your child. If he ends up being signed to a five-year, multi-gazillion-dollar contract twenty years down the road, that's terrific. But if he isn't, being realistic now will give him options.

At the most basic level, if your athlete continues his sport into his high school years, it's an extracurricular activity that will look good on college and/or employment applications. It may present job opportunities, such as coaching younger players or becoming a youth referee.

If he possesses talent and develops it, he may be able to parlay his sports ability into a college scholarship. However, don't stop putting money in his college fund just yet, because only a small percentage of high school athletes receive scholarships to college. If your child does end up making it as a college athlete, he has a chance—albeit a slim one—to move into the professional ranks (if his sport has one) when he graduates. Again, don't pin your hopes—or let him pin his—on sports as a career. Make certain he pursues a college major with career potential, and that he puts as much or more effort into it as he does his sport.

What about his dreams of making the Olympic Team? His chances of getting there are even more remote. But having said that, let us emphasize that there are athletes who do become Olympians, and, if your child has the talent and the drive, he just might end up being one of them.

If your child is one of those few truly gifted athletes who has a real shot at succeeding in his sport, you're going to face challenges that we SportsMoms of Mere Mortals won't. (Or you'll face some of the same challenges, but at a greater level of intensity.)

How much time will this hyper-dedication to his sport take? How will it affect other activities in his life—as well as your own? What impact will his sport have on your other children? Do you have the money to pay for advanced involvement in sports? How do you encourage him in his sport and at the same time lay groundwork so he's not devastated if he doesn't make the college, pro, or Olympic ranks?

If you end up being SportsMom to a superstar, you'll have to think about these and many other issues, then decide how you'll handle them. The most important—at least as far as we're concerned—is how you're going to raise your player so that his confidence as an athlete doesn't translate into arrogance as a human being.

If, on the other hand, you end up being one of us Mere Mortal SportsMoms, relax, enjoy the journey, and have fun.

PART TWO

Preparing to Participate

C h a p t e r   4

Getting Started

IF YOU'RE THE SPORTSMOM of a very young child who wants to participate in a sport at a beginner's level, getting started is pretty simple: in most instances, you just sign up and show up. But as time goes on and your athlete advances in his sport, or if he's older and trying out for a sport like high school football for the first time, he must undergo two rites of passage: trying out and practicing. You are in charge of getting him through both.

Tryouts

There are things in life that, struggle as we might to understand them, are shrouded in mystery, *e.g.,* programming a

VCR, understanding how the Internet works, and trying out for an organized youth sport. Be advised that you must undergo this latter mystery whether or not your child is taking part in a team or an individual sport.

It is your job to find out when tryouts will be held. Before you do, though, you must do some homework to find out which organizing body you and your child will feel most comfortable in. In most organized youth sports, you target the organizing body you want to be associated with, your child tries out, and the coach of an individual team within that organizing body decides if he wants your athlete: Coach chooses you; you don't choose Coach.

Depending upon the sport or team your child is interested in, the organizing body may take the form of the community recreation department, school athletic department, the Y, the rink, or local youth sports association. For our SportsMom parenting purposes, the organizing body also includes the other SportsMoms (and dads).

To learn about the organizing body, talk to other Sports-Moms and plug into the local grapevine, which is still one of society's most reliable sources of information.* What you should be looking for in an organizing body are officials and other parents who share your basic values and views on the role sports should play in a child's life. Generally speaking, if you're comfortable with the organizing body, Coach will be a pretty good fit, too.

Once you've determined the organizing body you want to be part of, ask when tryouts are being held—then brace yourself. If this is your first tryout, nothing can totally prepare

---

* For the SportsMom Grapevine™, see our Postscript ("P.S.") on page 183.

SportsMom™

© 1998 KBL

"Julie made the team! First meeting is Tuesday, 6 p.m. Bring your insurance card, her birth certificate, picture, release of liability form, registration forms, and your checkbook..."

either you or your athlete for what is ahead. Tryouts can be unpredictable, stressful, and very confusing. We're not telling you this to scare you, but to warn you that this experience—which most Rookie SportsMoms assume will be a walk in the park—can be anything but.

The first reason that tryouts can be problematic is that each coach does them a little differently. Again, talk to Veteran SportsMoms who know the coaches, and plug into the grapevine.

Another reason tryouts can be stressful is that you go in thinking that your child will try out, make the team, be able to play with his buddies, and you'll go on your merry way. You're basing that on your belief that your child is as good as the next kid who's trying out. However, that's not always the case.

Your child may be a whiz at math and charming as can be, but not be athletically blessed. Or, he may be good at the sport, but everyone else trying out is *very* good. He may even be very good, but Coach already has three players who can play his position and do it even better. Or, Coach is gearing up for a championship season, he's in the market for exceptional talent, and he's got the clout and reputation to fill all his slots with the *crème de la crème* of the entire community.

When that happens, you've got one unhappy camper on

your hands. Your child is disappointed that he didn't make the cut and upset that he can't play with his friends who did. How he learns to handle these trials is up to you. Allowing him to blame Coach, indulge in endless self-pity, or nurse a grudge will set behavioral patterns he'll likely follow throughout life. You may be tempted to let your seven-year-old get away with a "cute," even understandable, temper tantrum when he doesn't make the soccer team. However, how will that behavior be looked upon when he's forty years old and raging at his boss because he didn't get promoted? You may think we're stretching it here, but we don't.

Once you've dealt with the emotional aspects of disappointment, try to get your child involved in something else: another sport altogether or a different level of play at which he can succeed. You may want to look at non-sports activities. (We may be SportsMoms, but we recognize that there are lots of other interesting things kids can do.) Whatever you do, don't let him take all that enthusiasm he had before tryouts and throw it away. Help him channel it into an endeavor that builds his self-esteem and his character.

If your child made the team, your job is easier, but just as important. You need to make certain your child learns how to deal with his success, particularly if he has friends who didn't make the cut. He must learn to be sensitive to their disappointment, and look for ways to maintain their friendship through other activities.

Now, we'd like to discuss what we call *The Darker Side of Tryouts*. We want to emphasize that this Darker Side raises its ugly head only occasionally, but you need to keep your SportsMom antennae up to protect your child in case it does.

What we mean by the Darker Side is when your child doesn't make the team, not because he lacks talent, but because there's a dynamic to the selection process that isn't apparent. Maybe only kids from private schools make the cut.

Maybe only kids whose dads played high school football with Coach do. Maybe the moon is full. Who knows?

Certainly not you, because you're racking your brain to come up with a reason that's going to make sense to your disappointed child—and to you. Remember, though, that there are many times in life when there aren't clear-cut reasons for why things turn out the way they do. Helping your child understand and learn to cope with that fact is an Important Lesson of Life that will help him in the future. But we know it's tough.

We also want to talk about another dynamic that falls within the Darker Side. If you've earned a reputation for being difficult, either as a SportsMom on another team or in life in general, Coach may not pick your athlete because he doesn't want to have to deal with you. We cannot over-emphasize this reality: if you're obnoxious or whiny or otherwise unpleasant, you can—in fact, you will—negatively impact your child's sports experience.

If you're a Rookie SportsMom, that should be incentive enough to avoid annoying sideline behavior and unreasonable demands on Coach, as well as loathsome behavior at PTA meetings. If you've already got a reputation as a giant pain in the patoot, it's time to eat some crow, make amends, and change your evil ways, baby. There is so much in youth sports you can't control but your behavior is one thing you can, so do it for your kid's sake.

Practices

Practices are designed to help athletes learn new skills, perfect old ones, and, in team sports, acquire the "how-to's" of working together. When your child practices enough, game skills and strategies become second nature, sharpening his competitive edge.

Whether your child is pursuing an individual or team sport, there are certain things that you, as SportsMom, should be looking for in practices.

First, there should be an adult (or near-adult, *i.e.*, a coach in his late teens) who supervises every practice your child attends. If there's no adult in place when you arrive with your child, don't leave until one gets there. Remember: accidents happen, people get sick, and despite advances in telecommunications, Coach may not be able to reach you if he has to cancel at the last minute. Even the phone tree, a staple of youth sports, doesn't always work. Some teams post last-minute notices on a league website, but they're not much help for families without Internet access.

Coach should have a plan for every practice. This doesn't have to be written down or even very detailed; however, it should be apparent by watching practice that Coach has some goals in mind, and is taking steps to help his players meet them. Practice should be run in accordance with Coach's philosophy of the game. It should also be constructed in a way that safely conditions players' bodies. That means not only warm-up drills, but also allowances made for extreme heat, cold, and humidity, and individual player's medical conditions, plus cool-downs at the end.

Coach should also be sensitive to what's happened to his athlete(s) since the last practice. If there's just been a particularly ugly competition, Coach should take time to interpret the defeat and diffuse churning emotions. He may assign blame, but it should be fair, and he should also put a stop to any unfair blame leveled at one athlete by another.

We cannot overemphasize the importance of practices in your young athlete's life. This is where he can learn several Important Lessons of Life, including—

- The value of working with others
- How to set goals
- The steps necessary to achieve goals
- How to persevere when an endeavor becomes routine and boring
- How to meet new challenges

Some might say that competitions are where the rubber meets the road, and, in one sense, that's true. However, we believe that the "rubber" of your child's character "meets the road" in practice. It's easy to show up and play a game when the level of excitement is high; it's harder to dredge up the grit to grind through practice after practice. Stars may be born in games, but character is birthed in practice.

For that reason alone, you should make certain your child gets to practice on time, every time. Failing to do so under-mines the notion that he has an obligation to his teammates; in individual sports, it signals disrespect for Coach's time. In either case, your child is sacrificing an opportunity to learn and grow in his sport.

When your child is late for practice or fails to show, you chip away at the lessons you're trying to teach him about self-discipline and time management. You may even jeopardize your child's standing: many coaches have "no practice, no play" rules. We recognize that it isn't always possible for you to get your child to practice yourself. However, it is your responsibility to arrange a safe ride there and back. It's also your responsibility—on those occasions when you simply can't avoid being late—to communicate that fact to Coach in advance when possible or apologize afterward. This isn't just good manners: it's self-preservation, the kind that will keep you from falling victim to The Darker Side we mentioned earlier.

Finally, we come to a question many Rookie SportsMoms ask about practices: *Should I stay?*

That depends on your child's age, and the distance between practice and home.

If your child is very young and practice is short, you may want to stay. If your child is older, stay at least until the point you know an adult is on hand to supervise and your child is doing okay. Take cues from your player, too. You can tell by the look he's giving you if he wants you to sit on the sidelines or make tracks. If he wants you to leave but it's more convenient for you to stay, move as far away from the action as possible, and pay no attention to what's going on. This "invisible" SportsMom mode is excellent for short naps, catching up on bill paying, or escaping into the pages of a novel.

If your child is okay with your leaving and you live ten minutes away, the time he's at practice can be a great opportunity to return home to start supper or fold laundry before you pick him up. If your home is further away from practice, you may want to use the time to run errands, buy groceries, or leisurely (an adverb rarely associated with SportsMom) sip a cup of cappuccino at a local coffee shop.

Skill Development

Many a SportsMom automatically assumes that if she delivers her player to practice, Coach will be responsible for the ongoing development of her child's *individual* skills.

That is a realistic expectation in individual sports, such as tennis, gymnastics, or figure skating. Individual player development in team sports is a different story.

A good team coach should be interested in your child as a person, of course, but his primary job is to develop a *team*. If your player's individual skills improve in the process, that's terrific, but the prevailing belief in team sports is that the development of individual skills is pretty much up to your player and you.

Some coaches hold their own camps and clinics to help you; others can recommend good places to go for individual skill-building. A good coach will be happy to provide suggestions your child can pursue on his own by practicing at home. It's your job, SportsMom, to encourage and support that home practice, because that's what will make a difference in your child's level of play.

C h a p t e r 5

Child Growth and Development

Note: The information in this chapter is not intended as a substitute for professional medical advice.

IF YOUR CHILD PLAYS A SPORT—be it recreational or competitive—it's helpful for you to know about child growth and development. You need not pursue a Ph.D. in the subject to be up to the task: a working knowledge will go a long way in helping you know what your child thinks and feels at different stages of his life. It will also help you understand what you can—and can't—reasonably expect from him as he plays his sport.

Isn't This Coach's Job?

Some among you may be asking, "Why am I the one who needs to know about this? Shouldn't Coach be the one who knows this stuff, since he's the person controlling what the players do?"

You're not alone in your thinking. Most SportsMoms expect Coach to know about subjects—nutrition, training, child growth and development—that directly affect their children. However, reasonable as it may seem to you that Coach knows about this stuff, it may be difficult to find someone to fit the bill. Many teams have a hard enough time finding a coach who knows the game *and* has the skill, temperament, and organization to effectively guide young athletes through the season.

As SportsMom, you're ultimately responsible for the health and welfare of your child. If you're lucky enough to have a knowledgeable coach, he can help you. On the other hand, a coach who puts inappropriate physical or psychological demands on your kid can hamper your efforts, or even cause permanent damage.

Given this, it seems to us that the only alternative we SportsMoms have is to obtain a basic knowledge of child growth and development. If what you learn raises concerns about what is going on in your child's sport, discuss it privately with Coach. You may even wish to offer to share your resources with him, and/or make them available to other parents.

To get you started, we're going to spend the rest of this chapter covering some basics about child growth and development, plus a little bit on the difference between boys and girls. Please note that this information is by no means exhaustive: to learn more, hit your local library or bookstore.

Two Simultaneous Forces

As your child grows and develops, always remember that he has two simultaneous forces of change taking place in one body. First, he is growing and developing psychologically (self, mind, and soul). Second, he is growing and developing physiologically (bone, muscle, and internal organs).

Our society has long relied on play to help children gain control over their growing bodies, as well as to develop positive psychological characteristics and interpersonal skills. Today, once a child reaches school age, play is likely to take the form of organized sports.

Ages Five through Seven: A Bit Clumsy, and Totally Focused on "Me"

From ages five through seven, the average child grows three inches and gains ten pounds. Proportionately, his head is still the biggest part of his body. Imagine what it would be like to do sprints, hit a tennis ball, or kick a soccer ball if your head was twice its current size. Needless to say, expecting your player to be super coordinated at this age is expecting too much. Ditto for always keeping his balance as he runs the bases.

Psychologically, your five-to-seven-year-old athlete is *young*. And because he is young, he is self-centered and wants to keep whatever he is playing with to himself. He may be starting to understand cooperative play, but don't count on him to relate it to teamwork. That's why he won't throw the ball from the outfield to second base: the way he sees it, throwing the ball to someone else has nothing to do with the All-Important Me.

If you have a kid this age, you know he likes to boast about his accomplishments—and you probably feel awkward when it happens. You want him to recognize when he's done something well, but more than a little boasting feels like too much to you. However, that ain't necessarily so, because kids this age are still learning that they can make things happen, and boasting is their way of verbalizing that reality.

Eventually, your child should grow out of his need to brag excessively. In the meantime, intervene only if his boasting is based on his belief that he is better than someone else. At this age, your child is beginning to grasp how other people feel and perceive an event, so it's prime time to help him understand that feeling and acting superior hurts another person's feelings.

Because a five-to-seven-year-old is so self-centered, he misinterprets constructive criticism about his sports skills: he thinks you're criticizing him as a person. In other words, if you or Coach try to tell a child something was wrong with his performance on the field, he takes it to mean that you think something is wrong with *him.* He can't separate what he does from who he is, so concentrate on reinforcing what he does right, instead of harping on what he does wrong.

From age five to seven, your child's attention span is limited. He gets lost trying to follow detailed instructions. He may not know or understand certain words. To get your point across, limit directions, use simple language, and keep it short. Needless to say, this is no age for detailed plays or elaborate game plans.

Ages Eight though Ten: Beginning to Recognize and Value Relationships

If you're SportsMom to an eight-to-ten-year-old, you've probably seen that he's starting to develop the muscle strength to support more strenuous and sustained physical activity. You've no doubt noticed that the development of his body structure is uneven: his legs are probably too long for the rest of him right now. You've also discovered that growing pains aren't old wives' tales: sometimes your child's growth does result in very real aches and pains. And you are oh-so-aware that your child's uneven physical growth is matched by the uneven development of his maturity, concern for others, and overall judgment.

For example, six months ago he wanted you to display a reasonable amount of attention to the insignificant injuries that come with practicing and playing a sport. Now, in the face of those same injuries, your athlete is stoic, showing no hurt in front of his peers. Or, he carries on endlessly, demanding more compassion than the injury is worth.

He is also increasingly aware of his peer group. He knows that he is part of something bigger than himself. He has a sense of where he wants to fit in, because it is becoming important to be a part of something more than *Me.* He wants to hear about the good things the group accomplished, but he still prefers to hear about what he, specifically, did well. You may find, though, that he'd rather get his praise from his peer group than from you. That group has taken on a new importance in his life, and he's starting to look to it, not just you, for approval. Don't let this hurt your feelings, SportsMom, because it has nothing to do with you personally: it's a natural stage in child development.

You may have noticed that your eight-to-ten-year-old is beginning to organize his thoughts. That means he is gaining the ability to grasp a basic game plan, or understand a strategy Coach is emphasizing. He can also recall details about one game situation and apply them to others, which is something he couldn't do when he was younger. At this age, teamwork also starts to make sense to him: *So **that's** why I'm supposed to throw the ball to second base!* (You can almost see the light bulb clicking on over his head.)

Your child may like to organize his life around things that are familiar, but he's starting to see relationships between different events and ideas. Kids this age are very practical and pretty straightforward: your child likes to do, to try, and to be told that he did it well. You may not think so now, but someday—about the time he hits the high-drama years of mid-adolescence—you're going to look back on this period of your child's life as The Golden Age of Parenting.

Ages Eleven through Thirteen: Child One Day, Adult the Next

The early adolescent (ages eleven through thirteen) is somewhere 'twixt and 'tween. Although no age group exhibits a standard set of characteristics, this seems particularly true for young adolescents. No one becomes a teenager all at once. One day, your child is twelve going on forty; the next, he's displaying the emotional maturity of a two-year-old. He looks so grown up, and acts so childish. Wise one minute, foolish the next. Back and forth he lurches on the path from child to adulthood, seemingly without rhyme or reason.

SportsMom™

"But mom, you can't wash my uniform. It's lucky."

Physically, both boys and girls grow a lot at this stage, but girls change more because this is prime time for their advancement toward adulthood: boys' comes a bit later, around age fourteen. Although girls this age adopt teenage airs and interests while their male counterparts appear to lag behind, the truth is that both genders look and feel awkward during this period of their lives.

Up till this time, your athlete has been fairly comfortable with his body, but now his attitude is changing. He may have been a star runner last fall, but now his longer legs are giving him fits as he makes his way 'round the track. The always-slim little girl may develop a paunch until her height catches up with her recent weight gain. Kids this age need lots of reassurance. From your perspective, these changes are a natural part of growing: for your child, they can be traumatic.

This is an especially trying time for girls: their hormones have kicked in and the results are right out there for all the world to see. Her developing bosom gets in the way when she swings a bat or golf club, or bounces embarrassingly when she runs down the basketball court. Wider hips throw off her balance on the beam, or make a once-simple double axel a study in clumsiness. If you have a girl this age, SportsMom, she needs lots of support, both from you and a good sports bra.

The mindset and mental abilities of kids this age make them both easy and hard to parent and coach. Your young adolescent can think abstractly, link events, and see the purpose of plans. This is when game plans and strategy start to be fun. Your athlete also comprehends the relationship between practicing and the quality of his play. That does not mean, however, that he wants to repeat drills *ad infinitum*. He craves variety and looks for opportunities to try new approaches and skills, so you need to find ways to help make his home training more interesting.

However, his willingness to try something new is directly related to his view of himself. A kid this age who is still with a sport will likely view his experience as positive, and consider his abilities equal to its challenge, whether it's recreational or competitive. He also wants to meet everyone's expectations, but most importantly, his own.

This is tricky territory for a SportsMom or Coach to navigate. One minute, your young adolescent player sees himself as capable and competent. The next, he is complaining that he has failed, can't make the mark, and that no one around him appreciates what he does or how hard it is to do it.

This is where you have a very real parenting advantage over moms and dads who aren't involved in activities with their kids. As we said before, children this age start to pull away from their parents, preferring to spend more time with their peers. But youth sports require you to continue to spend lots of time together, held "car-captive" on the way to practices, competitions, and tournaments. While there's something to be said for spending quality time with your child, there's nothing like quantity time with nothing to do but shoot the breeze to get a kid talking.

> This is where you have a very real parenting advantage over moms and dads who aren't involved in activities with their kids.

When he does start spilling his guts about how he's feeling, we recommend avoiding long-winded speeches that focus on your view of the situation. He won't be listening anyway. Instead, help your athlete articulate his view of the situation. When the opportunity presents itself, slip in a little reality, then help him see what he can do to improve the situation. Your job here is to be like a good therapist: you don't tell him straight out what to do; you help him learn how to go through the process of discovering answers for himself.

SportsMom™

"Are we having quality time yet?"

However, you are allowed to steer him pretty strongly in the right direction.

Between ages eleven and thirteen, many kids choose to leave a sport. Given all the time, energy, and money you've invested, you may feel a real letdown. You may fear that he'll live to regret his decision just a few months down the road. You may be afraid that if you let him quit his sport, he'll give up on every important endeavor of his life.

Be honest with your player. Together, sort out the reality of the situation. Look for the real reasons he feels the way he does. Discuss alternative activities. And remember that sometimes quitting is okay. (See Chapter 9 for a discussion on quitting.) Above all, recognize this situation for what it is: an opportunity to help your child learn how to make rational, measured decisions about important issues that affect his life. Think of this as practice for the Big Game Called Life.

Experienced SportsMoms say that one thing that makes it easier to deal with young adolescents is that they usually have a good sense of humor and appreciate adults who have one, too. Appealing to your athlete's sense of humor can get you through a multitude of difficult situations. However, always remember that your young adolescent still tends to interpret remarks literally, particularly offhanded remarks meant to be funny. While this may seem to contradict the idea that he has begun to think abstractly, it doesn't: the sweet kid simply believes what you tell him. Enjoy it while it lasts.

Ages fourteen through Seventeen

Fourteen- to seventeen-year-olds, or older adolescents, are not a homogeneous group. The youngest in this group is a child just leaving middle school, while the oldest is a young adult preparing to leave high school. Within this group, skills and maturity levels vary widely.

However, one thing older adolescents do have in common is a strong desire to conform, or fit in. They want to look like each other and act like each other. That can be tough if they have trouble making connections with other kids, or if they don't possess the body *du jour*.

Obviously, your teen does not need critical remarks about his body, either from you or Coach. So don't make references to lingering baby fat or other perceived flaws, and head Coach off at the pass if he does. (Believe it or not, one of us once had a child on a team headed by a coach who steadily harassed another player because he was shorter than average. So yes, you may run into a coach with the sensitivity of an ox.) Even if you and Coach are sensitive souls, you should be aware that seemingly-innocent remarks may wound, heightening your child's insecurity. For example, your slender, willowy daughter may not appreciate admiring remarks about her height, because no one else on the team is as tall.

At this age, a player's size, speed, and skill make him physically vulnerable, so you and Coach must work together to make injury prevention a priority. (We'll talk about this more in Chapter 7.) You also need to know that your player's desperate desire to fit in may keep him in the game when he's hurt, or motivate him to get back in the game when a previous injury has not properly healed. It's your job to keep an eye on things to minimize the possibility of this happening.

Psychologically, this period in a child's life swings between quiet introspection and outrageous behavior. Adults who have experience coaching this age group are usually sensitive to its wildly-vacillating rhythms; if this is your first go-round as a SportsMom to a kid this age, hang onto your hat.

One thing you should always keep in mind is that older adolescents are usually having a crisis. Teen girls are particularly adept at drama. As SportsMom, you must act as a sympathetic sounding board during these times, providing just enough feedback (and not one iota more) to help your teen give the situation a sense of proportion.

Actually, it's easy to understand why everything seems like a crisis to your child. He's in the final pre-adult stages of learning to live responsibly and handle relationships. His increasing academic load is a preview of adult responsibilities to come. His sports involvement places him in very competitive situations where he's expected to perform well. And, if that weren't enough, he's learning to cope with the hormones that are raging through his body. It's a lot to handle, and sometimes it overwhelms him.

It's also customary for kids this age to be given more and more independence. This is part of the process of becoming self-reliant young adults. Children who excel in athletics are often expected to handle this independence very early and especially well. However, expecting athletic maturity to translate directly into real-life maturity is a mistake. Being a top-seeded tennis player, a valuable intramural point guard, or a gold-medal figure skater does not mean he will automatically make mature decisions in other areas of life.

Ditto for assuming or demanding maturity based on your child's looks. She may be fully developed and wear shoes larger than yours, but you have to remember that her adult body houses a fifteen-year-old child, with all her foibles and insecurities. You may need to quietly remind Coach of that sometimes, and you will certainly have to remind your child: when she looks into the mirror and sees an adult staring back at her, she may think she can handle it all.

One of the most difficult things your older teen faces at this point in his life is standing up to his peers in order to do the right thing, particularly when it comes to alcohol, drugs, and sexual activity. Although many of us SportsMoms got our kids involved in sports in order to provide them with a positive alternative to these negative behaviors, we must realize that athletes are presented with the same opportunities to indulge as other high schoolers. Plus, many athletes are subtly encouraged to cross boundaries and exceed limits as a typical function of pursuing sports; while this may not have been intended to encourage involvement in negative activities, the pattern of pushing limits—and enjoying it— has been established.

When your child faces serious temptations, it's your job to be there to help him make good decisions. However, you must lay the groundwork for this years ahead of his teens: start talking to him early and often about drugs and alcohol, then, when appropriate, about sex. Encourage him to come to you with questions. Do that enough, and he'll continue to come to you when he's in his teens. Don't act shocked or upset, no matter what he asks. Research shows that kids with parents who talk about these difficult subjects are much less likely to get involved in risky behaviors. (Remember: you have all that time in the car.)

Coach also plays an important role in the older teen's life. He is an adult, but he is different from a parent, and often, in the teen's mind, more important to please. That's why it is vital that you find a coach with the right fit for you, your child, and your values. At this age in particular, SportsMom and Coach must be on the same page when it comes to academic issues, standards of behavior, and moral values. You cannot undo Coach, and Coach cannot undo you, without confusing your child.

By the time your child reaches the fourteen-to-seventeen-year-old age group, he has probably had years of experience in athletics. He's comfortable with the demands of his sport, and is learning that he can become an even better player by building on his foundation of basic skills. All in all, not a bad Lesson of Life to be learned. If he's on the upper-age limit of the group, there's a good chance he's informally mentoring one of the younger kids in the group, learning, in the process, the very adult job of passing on important information to others. That's the upside of athletics and older teens.

The downside is that the move to high school sports or more competitive situations may mean that someone will be left behind. For the first time ever in your child's athletic career, either he or one of his friends may not make the cut.

This takes a serious toll on SportsMom and her athlete. If your child is cut, don't rush in like an overzealous cheerleader intent on banishing his sadness: instead, let him have a moment to feel the disappointment. Just don't let him—or you—get stuck in it. Then, help him remember that there are a lot of different sports, and the pleasure of playing something new can help diminish the sorrow he's feeling. You'll be helping him learn that life is full of trade-offs: the ability to see other possibilities in the face of disappointment or adversity is part of becoming an adult.

On the other hand, if your child is not cut, but his friend is, you can teach him the importance of supporting people he cares for when they go through tough times. Depending upon his sensitivity to others—or lack thereof—it may also be time to teach him how to be gracious in victory.

If your child is very talented and skilled, he may be called upon to make some serious decisions about sports between the ages of fourteen and seventeen. If he plays several sports, he may be asked to concentrate his energies on that one in which he particularly excels. He may be asked to give up a sport he likes because it builds the wrong type of muscles for the sport to which he's truly committed. Increased focus on one sport may prevent him from participating in other extracurricular activities. It may limit time with his friends. You need to be there to guide him through these new experiences and steer him in the direction of good decisions.

If you and your child determine that he does not want to pursue his sport at a higher level, you must protect him from feeling he does not measure up to expectations—his, yours, Coach's, or society's in general. Although many talented players gain a lot from stepping up their commitment to a sport, many others who pass on the opportunity go on to fulfill their potential in other areas. It's largely up to you to guide your child through this experience. As we've said many other times, you know your child better than anyone, so trust your instincts, help him make his decision, and refuse to indulge in "what-if's." Learning to make decisions and move on confidently is another one of those Lessons of Life SportsMoms live for: teach him this one by example.

The Difference Between Boys and Girls

Now that we've touched on some basic developmental issues, we want to address the differences between boys and girls.

Based on our personal experience as moms to both genders, we feel safe in saying that boys and girls are very different creatures through all the ages and stages of childhood and adolescence. Lest we be misunderstood, let us establish up front that we are big believers in equality of opportunity for girls and boys in sports. What we do not believe is that the experience is identical, or the same, for both.

We realize that some people will disagree with us. It's our observation, though, that a girl's biology and its natural difference from a boy's biology cannot be explained away as a gender equity issue. We believe that there are very real differences between boys and girls that make their sports experience somewhat different—and science appears to back us up on this.

Recently, the study of sex hormones and brain structure has revealed slight, but very real differences in men and women. These differences influence spatial perception that impacts eye-hand coordination, and mechanical and social abilities that affect fine motor skills. Different, too, is the ability to pay attention and concentrate, as well as language areas of the brain that influence reading and speaking.

If you've ever worked with preschool or young children, this is hardly news. What's important about the information is how we, as SportsMoms, use it. Although sports is often viewed as a good place to help a child learn gross motor skills or learn to pay attention, we must realize that boys and girls develop these skills at different times and rates. We must adjust our expectations accordingly, and we must learn never to compare.

Girls and boys have very different views on issues that pertain to sports. Research indicates that girls like to participate in sports for the *esprit de corps,* or the simple goal of competing. Boys may be more enamored with the physicality of grinding opponents into the dirt, and winning.

As early as first grade, girls are more negative about their athletic ability than boys are. Girls are not certain they really want to push themselves in the same manner that boys do: some researchers suggest that this is because boys have been encouraged to feel up to the task, while girls have not.

Boys forget, while girls remember—forever. So, when Coach makes a disparaging, off-the-cuff remark to a boys' team, he can assume his players are over it before practice is done. If he makes the same remark to a girls' team, he can assume his players will remember it through the entire season and into the next; in fact, they'll *remind* each other.

Although no sport is the exclusive province of males or females, girls and boys soon establish views on which sports are masculine or feminine. Each child's outlook is based on his own experience, his parent's views, and the opinion of the other people who are significant in his life. As SportsMom, you will, no doubt, influence your child's view of which sports are appropriate for men and which, for women. Whether you believe all sports are fair game for either sex, or whether you believe that some are not appropriate for one gender or another, you should stress that girls and boys deserve an equal opportunity to participate in some type of sport. Too many of us remember a time when boys' sports got all the money and attention, and girls teams—if there were any—embroidered the school mascot on sweatshirts and called them uniforms.

Of course, no matter what you say, your player will probably pursue what he wants. However, there is ample opportunity to intervene in the early years, when the hard and fast view of gender-appropriate roles is less firmly entrenched. Girls do not have to assume passive, weak roles; boys do not have to take on only assertive and strong roles. Girls should be encouraged to assert themselves and boys should be encouraged to talk about their feelings; however, this is not Coach's job, but yours.

Be alert to the subtle and not-so-subtle ways your player's participation in sports may be undermined by gender expectations. We're not just talking to the parents of girls here; watch out for any negative that impacts your child, be your athlete he or she. Let your athlete know that you appreciate the special skills he brings to the game, and, most importantly, that you value the time you get to spend together.

As SportsMoms, we believe our goal should not be to make sports equal by androgyny. Our goal, whether our player is male or female, is to make certain that sports *per se* play an important role in our player's maturation and overall childhood/adolescent experience.

SportsMom™

© 1998 KBL

MONSTER BURGER

"Go ahead, Mom, splurge."

Good Nutrition: Fueling Your Player Properly

REMEMBER HEALTH CLASS in high school? One of the things you undoubtedly learned about was nutrition, and how important it is to eat right. Since becoming a mom, you may have boned up a bit more on what kids need to eat to grow and function properly.

But now you're SportsMom, and if you're like most women who take on the role, you have new concerns about nutrition and your child. You may wonder if the physical demands of his sport require special kinds of food or vitamins. You question how you can carve out time in your wild and crazy SportsMom schedule to prepare nutritious meals like you used to (or wish you used to). Your increasing dependence on fast food may have you fearing your child thinks the four basic food groups are burgers, fries, chicken nuggets, and shakes.

This chapter is designed to provide you with some basics on nutrition and sports, offer suggestions on working good nutrition into your jam-packed life, and briefly address such nutritional negatives as anorexia and bulimia.

Nutrition is Fuel

Think of nutrition as the power supply your child needs to build and operate his body.

Notice that we said *nutrition*, not *food.* Loosely defined, food is anything you can put in your mouth that won't

immediately kill you and that you can digest. Nutrition refers to those substances that nourish the body. Nutrition is food, but food is not always nutrition (think cotton candy*), and that, SportsMom, is what has you worried. Sure, your player is eating, but is what he's eating giving him the nutrients he needs, particularly now that he's playing a sport?

You are right to be concerned, because the development of your child's body is absolutely reliant on what goes into it to

---

* Lest we get angry letters from the Cotton Candy Association of America, let us be clear that we are not anti-cotton-candy. However, like other sweets, it is best enjoyed as an occasional treat, rather than as a diet staple.

meet its basal metabolic requirements. And, as you suspected, your athletic child does have special energy requirements. However, unless your child has an extremely grueling training regimen, the basics of good nutrition and a measure of SportsMom good sense will fulfill them.

Nutritional Basics

The basics of good nutrition start with a balanced diet. This does not mean *diet* the way we use it most often in our culture, *i.e., weight-loss diet.* When we say *diet,* we mean the right combination of foods that ensure your child's growth, energy, and well-being, and hopefully, establish lifelong healthy eating patterns. We think it's interesting that the word *diet* comes from a Greek word meaning *a way of life.* As we're trying to teach our kids good nutrition, we certainly hope it turns out that way.

A balanced diet is constructed with four basic nutritional building blocks: protein; carbohydrates; fat; and vitamins and minerals.

Protein is *the* source for the structural development of your child's body, and is obtained by eating meat, milk, poultry, fish, cheese, dried beans, or nuts. Protein helps make cells, the tiny pieces of the body that combine to make your child grow, his brain think, and his blood bleed.

Proteins do provide energy, but are not immediately available as energy sources. Instead, protein serves as a source of energy when more-readily-available carbohydrate sources have been reduced. Proteins are most often called into play during athletic activities that require endurance: they are the body's deep-from-within energy source to delay fatigue.

Fat, despite the current bad rap it suffers, is also a necessary nutritional building block. Fat itself is not bad; it's just that too much fat (or the wrong kind) in the diet can be bad. In fact, fat is essential for your child's brain to function. ("So that's the problem," you're saying to yourself as you ponder your child's recent spate of absentmindedness. "Not enough fat!")

Fats can come from animals (butter, cream, lard) or plants (corn, olive, or canola oil). Generally speaking, fats from plants are better for you than fats from animals, and fats that are liquid at room temperature, better than fats that remain solid at room temperature.

Carbohydrates are the body's supreme energy source. That's because carbohydrates are either sugars or starches that are easily broken down by the body into glucose, then sent directly into the bloodstream to fuel the body, or stored for later use. The body's process of breaking down other sources of energy, such as protein, into usable glucose takes more time and energy. Carbohydrates come from foods like pasta, beans, rice, bread, cereal, and potatoes.

Vitamins and Minerals round out the nutritional mix. They help keep the body's enzymes, hormones, and metabolism working properly. If your child eats a balanced diet and reasonable amounts of food, he will get the vitamins and minerals he needs, even if he's added the physical demands of a sport to his routine.

What about vitamin and/or mineral supplements? If your child's eating right, he probably doesn't need them, but then again, a multivitamin pill isn't going to hurt him either. Megadoses aren't required, even for athletes, because when your child has too much of a vitamin or mineral, it is either

SportsMom™

"So like, Mom, what happened to all the rocky road ice cream?"

stored in body fat or excreted by his kidneys. We recognize that there are lots of different viewpoints on vitamins, so if you have questions, ask your pediatrician.

Bye-Bye, Fab Four: Hello, Pyramid

When we grew up, a balanced diet was based on eating the proper amounts of foods from each of what were called "The Four Food Groups." Within the past few years, however, the Nutritional Powers That Be have introduced a new, improved

The Food Pyramid

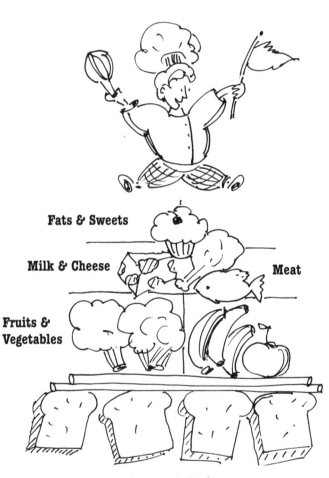

Fats & Sweets

Milk & Cheese   Meat

Fruits &
Vegetables

Cereals & Grains

Food Group Required Servings— Real-Life Translation

Fats and Sweets
☑ Use sparingly

Milk & Cheese
☑ 4 servings a day
Serving examples: 1 cup milk; 1 oz. cheese

Meat (Eggs, lean meat, fish, poultry, dried beans, peanut butter)
☑ 3 servings a day
Serving examples: 1 egg; 1 oz. beef or pork; 1 Tbsp. peanut butter; $\frac{1}{3}$ cup cooked dried beans

Fruits & Vegetables
☑ 4 or more servings a day, 1 of which is high in Vitamin C and 1 of which is high in Vitamin A.
- Citrus fruits and acidic veggies like tomatoes are a good source of Vitamin C.
- Green and yellow fruits and vegetables are a good source of Vitamin A.
- Don't overdo the starchy vegetables, like potatoes, corn, and lima beans.

Serving examples: 1 apple; $\frac{1}{2}$ banana or pear; 1 orange; $\frac{1}{2}$ cup cooked veggies; 1 cup raw veggies; $\frac{1}{2}$ cup fruit juice; $\frac{1}{4}$ cup raisins

Cereals & Grains (Enriched or whole grain cereals; bread; pasta; rice)
☑ 4 servings a day
Serving examples: $\frac{3}{4}$ cup cereal; 1 slice bread; $\frac{1}{2}$ cup cooked pasta; $\frac{1}{3}$ cup cooked rice

approach to a balanced diet called "The Food Pyramid." (We still jest about the four food groups being burgers, fries, chicken nuggets, and shakes because we have yet to come up with a good pyramid joke.)

If you develop and follow through on a straightforward nutrition game plan based on the Food Pyramid you see on page 82, you will be providing your child with everything he needs to grow and function properly.

What About Calories?

It is true that young athletes need more calories than children who are not physically active. Depending on the level of physical exertion, training, and practice frequency, they require 100 to 500 extra calories a day. (Ask your pediatrician about the required number of baseline calories for your child: it varies by age.) This is a general rule of thumb, influenced by the age and size of the child. The most important thing to remember is to supply those extra calories with the best nutritional bang for your calorie buck. You do not want your player to get his 500 calories from sugared soft drinks or high-fat snacks.

The ingredient labels on food packages, especially those on snacks purported to be healthy, can be a real assist in this area. It may seem logical to hand your kid a couple of all-natural, organic, no-artificial-anything snack bars—until you read the ingredients, see the high-saturated-fat content, and notice that the two bars your child needs to fill his tummy contain a whopping 500 calories. Also, don't be lulled by the fact that those bars came from the health food store: the ingredients may be terrific, but "health food" can be high in calories.

In dealing with kids and calories, always let your good SportsMom sense be your guide. Dieting is commonplace in America, and, unfortunately, children at increasingly younger ages are becoming preoccupied with having the perfect body, whatever that may be. Don't let your child become obsessed with calories, and don't give into that obsession yourself. Instead, set a positive tone that will help your child develop a lifelong attitude of enjoying good food for the right reasons. Always remember that food is fuel. While it's true that it should not become a child's emotional support system, it is also not his enemy.

Water, Water Everywhere

By weight, a child's body is sixty to seventy percent water. Proportionately speaking, kids have more body surface than adults, which means they have more skin through which to lose fluid. Although children perspire openly less than adults, they need more fluids than adults. If your child spends an hour or two in the hot sun without replenishing his fluid supply, he'll become dehydrated, and his concentration, endurance, coordination, and strength will suffer.

When it comes to fluids and your child, think quantity. Start with a base of five to eight glasses a day, and insist on more during training and practice. Although advertisers push the benefits of sports drinks, water ought to be the beverage of choice. It's good, it's plentiful, and—unlike much involved in youth sports—it's free (unless you prefer the bottled variety.) You may want to indulge your kid's desire to quaff certain sports drinks, but we think that water should predominate overall.

Water also has another advantage: it makes life simpler! You can find it almost everywhere, it isn't sticky when it's spilled on your vehicle's upholstery, you can use it to clean off a kid's scraped knee, or pour it over his head for a quick cool-down. Try that last move with a bottle of Gatorade® and see where it gets you!

One fluid we strongly recommend you limit is sugared soft drinks. First, these are empty calories without any valuable nutrients. Second, our experience has been that our players end up thirstier in the long run when they drink them. Finally, when your athlete drinks too much straight-up sugar, he'll get a sugar rush.

That's because straight-up sugar overwhelms the body's insulin system, which normally moves glucose (food energy in a usable form) from the blood to a storage system within the body. When your child drinks a sugared soft drink, his circulating blood is full of sugar, so it supplies his body with an overload of immediate energy. In response, his body signals for more insulin to move the sugar to storage. The body responds by supplying more insulin, which then takes glucose out of circulation, and your player is exhausted for lack of glucose. This is reason enough to avoid sugared soft drinks, and it's also why sugary snacks are not a good idea, either.

Making Good Nutrition Work, or a "Get Real" Meal Plan for SportsMoms

About now you may be thinking, "All this talk of nutrition is great, and I'd really like to do it right, but just how in the heck am I supposed to get balanced meals on the table when I'm juggling the Schedule from Hell?"

Good question, SportsMom, and one we asked ourselves once upon a time.

The answer is that you need a plan based on your own style of handling day-to-day kitchen detail. If you're not the grind-your-own-flour, bake-your-own-bread type, this is no time to start. Nor is all lost, nutritionally speaking, if you're the Queen of Take-Out. You can fit good nutrition into your way of doing things, as long as you have a strategy that takes the guesswork out of what to eat. That strategy will not only save your sanity when the pressure's on; it will benefit your athlete, your family, and you by making certain you're getting the nutrients you need to handle the chaos.

So you have to take the time to develop your plan and believe in it. Your effort on the front end will provide that bonus on the back end—where you need it the most.

The place to start is your pantry and freezer. Do you have the basics covered? Basic food items are quick, easy to prepare, and filling. How you define *basic food item* depends on your family's preferences, your culture/ethnicity, and your day-to-day kitchen detail style. Basics can range from peanut butter to capers, tomato soup to tomatoes pureed, or ranch dressing to a wine vinaigrette. The basics can serve as a foundation for fancier fare by adding simple spices, fresh vegetables, canned tomatoes, creamed soups, or cheese.

No matter what your style, we recommend adding these items to the basics:

- **Minced garlic.** Yes, Gourmet SportsMom, it is okay to use the already-prepared kind that needs to be refrigerated after opening. It can make plain taste special. Plus, it can be used with butter to create garlic bread, or added to meat or chicken to enhance its flavor.
- **Spaghetti sauce.** Homemade or canned, it does not matter, as long as it can cover pasta or pizza crust, or your kids can dip breadsticks into it.
- **Cheese.** Cheese can be used to top make-at-home pizza, make grilled cheese sandwiches, add protein to salads, or cut up for snacks. Keep in mind that shredded melts faster, but has a shorter shelf life. (Use the little bit of shredded left by mixing it with mayonnaise, spreading it on bagels, and sticking them under the broiler.)
- **Eggs.** A meal in themselves, eggs can also be deviled for snacks or mixed with milk for french toast.
- **Salad greens.** A stand-alone side dish with dressing, bagged salad greens can also serve as the foundation of a chef salad, or be added to tacos and sandwiches to fill them out.
- **Canned soup.** The age-old way to supplement a skimpy meal the night before the big grocery shop, canned soup can also serve as a snack or dinner. Chicken noodle soup rounds out a sandwich and creamed soups can add the right touch to not-quite-enough-rice-to-go-around.
- **Frozen vegetables and frozen, instant, or real mashed potatoes.** With the extras such as garlic, butter, margarine, sour cream, and salt and pepper, they can be a meal in

themselves. They can also give color and substance to that little bit of leftover chicken from last night.

- **Tortillas.** A great substitute for bread and noodles, tortillas turn into a sandwich with cheese and greens. Add chicken and sour cream and you have a casserole.
- **Cereal.** It's not just for breakfast anymore. It's a simple and quick something that hits the spot.

Once you've armed yourself with your version of the basics and these supplemental items, keep these tips in mind:

- Don't make it harder than it has to be. If you do not enjoy detailed recipes and your family appreciates boxed macaroni and cheese more than homemade pasta primavera, don't feel guilty about ripping open that little blue box.
- If you like to fly by the seat of your pants when it comes time to feed your family, the basics in your cupboard have to be there. If not, your budget's going to pay for your lack of planning via more restaurant meals or take-out.
- If you're a born organizer, plan out your meals for a four to five-week period, make one humongous shopping trip, then have a *cook and freeze* weekend like you read about in women's magazines. All you must do then is make a short trip to the grocer's once a week for milk and fresh fruit and vegetables to supplement the *thaw du jour.*
- Once a week, look ahead at your calendar and identify those days when the demands on your time will reach critical mass—then make a plan. Lay in a supply of food items that are easy to mix and match and have a fairly long shelf life. This is the time to use those easy-to-fix items your family likes—frozen pizza, pre-made subs—

that can be nutritionally supplemented with other easy items, like fruit and milk.

Our personal approach to providing our athletes and families with nutritious meals is a combination of all of the above. We think it provides maximum flexibility. But you should pick the style that best suits you and your family.

No matter which style you choose, one thing is for sure: you will not get away with being unprepared. Your plan may be detailed; it may be as simple as having a mental list of nutritious take-out meals you can afford. But whatever your plan, you must have one. Otherwise, your stress level will rise, your children will go hungry, your budget will get out of whack, and these issues will eventually reach a crisis level that takes far more time to handle than putting a plan together would have.

A good plan helps meet your athlete's nutritional requirements and also offers a bonus: you gain time you just might be able to spend doing something you like. Now there's a concept!

(One note of caution: while we firmly believe that your children should help with meal preparation, you must orchestrate and direct the overall plan. Children can be assigned age-appropriate tasks, such as setting the table, washing vegetables, pouring milk, even doing some of the actual cooking as they grow older. However, kids are not well-versed in nutrition and food handling. They should not be expected to go it alone without your direction.)

Meal Suggestions for Every SportsMom Style

We've already noted that you need to adapt your current style of handling kitchen detail to your jam-packed SportsMom schedule. Here are some suggestions designed to help:

Plain Food SportsMom

While it's not currently cool to admit you like plain food, the truth is that fancy food is just plain food dressed up— and no one likes to dress up every day all day.

We define *plain food* as a meal that requires no more than one pan to make, can be made anytime from the basics in your cupboard or fridge, and which requires only simple condiments and spices to add your personal touch. Examples:

Plain Food Breakfasts
- scrambled eggs, juice, and toast
- oatmeal, fruit, and yogurt
- pancakes or french toast and an orange

Plain Food Lunches
- baked potato, a salad, and a cookie
- grilled sandwich with lunchmeat and cheese, carrot sticks, and an apple
- pizza and a frozen fruit juice bar

Plain Food Suppers
- chili, salad, and fruit
- chicken, mashed potatoes, and sliced tomatoes
- hamburg or hotdog, bun, lotsa onions, with a mix of fresh fruit on the side

Grab-and-Go SportsMom

Grab-and-go foods require minimal preparation, no more than two hands to manage, and can be eaten without utensils: their remains are easily tossed into the nearest garbage pail. They can be eaten for breakfast, lunch, or dinner. Accompany with simple fluids, like bottled water, juice in a box, or milk in a carton. Add a piece of fresh fruit or a favorite vegetable and you have a complete nutritional package. Examples:

- a smoothie, which is milk, yogurt, fruit, wheat germ (optional) blended together
- bagel with cream cheese
- last night's pizza
- milkshake with strawberries and toast
- tortilla chips, melted cheese, and salsa
- any simple sandwich
- toasted English muffin, peanut butter and jelly

Take-Out SportsMom

The usual resource for take-out is the fast-food restaurant. While an occasional fast-food foray can keep you on time and fed, a steady diet of burgers and fries should not be your solution for every meal, every day. The combination of too much fat and sugar may fill your child's tummy, but it won't build muscle efficiently.

If you like the convenience of take-out and you can handle the cost, expand your take-out horizons. If you have a favorite restaurant but don't have time to visit it for a sit-down meal, call ahead and ask if they'll put together a meal for pick up. Collect the business cards of restaurants you go to, keep them in the car, and then, in desperate moments, call ahead to pick up a meal on the way home.

You can also employ ways to cut the cost. Call ahead for the main course, but skip the pricey salads and desserts: you can add those at home with ready-made, but cheaper items. Order just water to drink.

If you have time, pick up meals at lunch time when they're cheaper, store them in the fridge till dinner, then nuke them. Order large-size quantities rather than individual meals: buckets of spaghetti, pans of lasagna, quarts of soup. Freeze any leftovers for another meal.

Ahead-of-the-Curve SportsMom

Remember earlier when we mentioned having a *cook-and-freeze* day? This may be the ideal meal game plan for those of you who 1) like to organize your life for maximum efficiency; and/or 2) are really into regular home-cooked meals.

This strategy requires you to plan a month's worth of

meals—and a shopping list to match. Knowing what you're going to eat for the next thirty days eliminates what's often the toughest part of meal preparation: knowing what to make for dinner.

Start by deciding what you are in the mood for. If you have not had soup in a while and chicken salad also sounds good, start to organize your meal plans around these items. Make sure that your menu does not cluster the same general foods together over and over again to the point that your kids start feeling they're eating the same meal several days running, *i.e.*, *"This again, Mom?!"*

Here are some ideas that you may want to keep in mind as you make your menu plan:

- Bake three chickens. That night, serve one with the traditional mashed potatoes and mixed vegetables. Bone the other two. Use the meat for chicken salad and chicken enchiladas or tacos, add it to a pre-packed chicken pot pie that needs a bit more of the good stuff, or add it to the soup you've made from the chicken bones and leftover veggies. Eat the chicken salad the next night while it's fresh. The soup and enchiladas can go in the freezer for use at different times in the month.

- Marinate and grill two to three flank steaks. Serve up one with baked potatoes. The next day, use another to make fajitas by throwing in some peppers, onions, zucchini, and tomatoes. Prepare enough flank steak and you can use some in a stir-fry to be frozen for use later, or freeze some meat for sandwiches.

- Recycle the leftover ham you made for a special dinner. Create a hearty bean soup or scalloped potatoes. Add ham to salad for a complete meal. Use ham slices for sandwiches or serve them with eggs for a special breakfast.

- Turn five pounds of ground beef into hamburgers, meatloaf, chili, and spaghetti sauce. Form the hamburgers ahead, separate with wax paper and freeze. Mix up the meatloaf and freeze it. Serve the chili with tortillas and salad, then freeze the other half for a chili and french bread supper later in the month. Ditto for the spaghetti sauce.

Once you've planned your meals and done your mega-shopping, designate a day to cook. Don't allow anything to get in the way or you will find yourself with a refrigerator full of food—all of it close to its expiration date.

Menus based on cook-and-freeze days work best when they include a variety of different meals. In other words, don't turn that five pounds of ground beef into chili only to be eaten five times in a single month. And don't turn your well-thought-out plan into an inflexible routine that your family can use to remember the day of the week: *Mmmhhh, hotdogs: it must be Tuesday.*

If your family is of the vegetarian persuasion, you can adapt many of the suggestions we've made. Use cheese, eggs, soy, and fish for protein, or combine grains and beans to cover your protein requirements. As you well know, vegetarians must be a bit more attentive to make sure they're meeting their nutritional requirements, so you must keep an eye on the overall composition of your athlete's vegetarian diet.

Feeding a Team

If you are facing the prospect of feeding your child's fellow athletes at a team meal or on the road, remember these three rules:

1. Make it easy to prepare or purchase.
2. Make it easy to stretch to feed a few more.
3. Make it even easier to clean up.

When you think team meals, think sub sandwiches, pizza, tacos, chili, hamburgers, hot dogs, pasta, casseroles, nachos, salad, pancakes, cookies, cake, ice cream cones, watermelon, cut up apples, orange slices, and Jell-O® in a cup. Figure how much a serving of each item is, then multiply it by the number of people you're going to feed. Examples:

Item	One Serving	People	Need	Buy
Pizza	2 slices	32	64 slices	8 pizzas (8 slices per pizza)
Burgers	One patty	32	32 patties	8 lbs. of burger (4 patties per lb.)
Hot dogs	2	32	64 hot dogs	8 packages (8 dogs per pack)

When you're making your calculations, don't assume that every family eats the way you do. Your kids may eat two slices of pizza, but someone else's may eat four, so ask around. Too many kids and not enough pizza is *not* a pretty picture, SportsMom. On the other hand, you don't want to have so much extra that you're wasting food and money.

Family Time

In the rush to get nutritious food on the table (or at least into your family's collective stomach), don't forget the importance of shared mealtime. Sure, there are times when you can't all sit down together, but work to make these the exception rather than the rule.

Remember to use mealtime to discuss your lives, share your day, smile, laugh, and generally stay connected. Don't require every meal to be an event or expect every meal to be an opportunity to parent, though. There are times when it is more than enough that all of you are sitting down in one place at the same time.

Good Nutrition Before the Game

Even if they're old hands at good nutrition, many Rookie SportsMoms wonder if there are specific guidelines to follow immediately before their child practices or competes. Here are our best tips:

- Remember: your player's body uses the energy from food eaten one to four hours before exercise.
- Avoid serving a huge meal: a sandwich is a better idea. Something as simple and fast as a bowl of cereal will fill his stomach, but not slow him down.
- Before the game, make it low-fat: for example, serve chicken tacos, and hold the burrito with cheese and sour cream for later. Fat before the game can upset your player's stomach.
- Insist that your player drink water—lots and lots of it.
- Think carbohydrates: the complex kind includes foods like bagels and whole-wheat pretzels; the simple kind includes fruits.

The tip on carbohydrates may raise another question in your mind: *What's all this I hear about carbohydrate loading before competition, and does it apply to my child?*

Carbohydrate loading is a way athletes—usually at the college or professional level—meet the body's need for energy during sustained high-endurance activity, such as marathons and Ironman competitions.

Normally, the body stores enough energy (in the form of glucose) for 90 to 120 minutes of exercise. By consuming massive amounts of carbohydrates (which will be turned into glucose) three to four days prior to an event, the athlete is ensuring that he has extra energy upon which the body can draw. It's like not only filling your gas tank before a very long trip, but also hooking up reserve gas tanks you can tap into as needed when your standard tank runs low.

Young athletes do not need this mega load of carbohydrates: however, they can benefit from foods on the lighter side of "carbo load," eaten in reasonable quantities. Although your player doesn't need to wolf down carbs like a marathoner, you can still call it *carbohydrate loading* to keep him happy.

How Do You Know If Your Child Is Eating Right?

There are Wise Moms who start their children on the rosy path of good nutrition beginning with their first spoonful of solid food, insisting that they eat, not just what they like, but what is good for them.

Then there are The Rest Of Us. We applaud those Wise Moms. We envy them, too. Because while they never have to worry if their kids are eating right, we do. And when we become SportsMoms, we worry even more about the increased demands sports are putting on their growing bodies. So, if you're among The Rest Of Us, how do you tell if your child is eating right?

It's really quite simple: if your child is growing normally, it's a sign his nutritional needs are being met. If he has energy to enjoy life, his skin and hair look good, and he has no more than the average number of colds each year, he's probably getting what he needs, and you have a baseline on which to measure your child's nutrition.

If, on the other hand, he leaves certain foods on his plate, is always tired, or has other miscellaneous health complaints that have you suspecting he's getting insufficient protein, vitamins, or minerals, it's time to fine-tune your nutritional plan. If necessary, consult an expert who can develop a specific plan for your child. Your child's doctor should be able to give you the name of a reliable dietitian who specializes in pediatric nutrition.

As you observe your child (or your refrigerator), you'll certainly notice your child's growth spurts. Gallons of milk and boxes of cereal will disappear faster than you can say, "Who ate the...?" In particular, teenage boys are real food vacuums, so be prepared if you currently house one. Have healthy snacks he likes on hand; just don't expect to have them on hand too long.

Serious Trouble in NutritionVille*

As you observe your child's growth and development, keep your eyes open for signs of eating disorders, SportsMom. Is he too thin? Is his hair dull? Does he fatigue easily? Does he refuse even his favorite foods? Has he gone from enthusiastic exercise to exercising all the time? Pay attention, because anorexia nervosa and bulimia are at an all-time high, even among young athletes.

Unfortunately, we are raising our children in a world that is obsessed with appearance, and which considers anything more than too thin to be too heavy. Girls are more likely to succumb to the pressure to be thin than are boys, but eating disorders are not just the province of females. And, although

---

* Although anabolic steroids sometimes come in the form of nutritional supplements, we will address their dangers in our next chapter, which deals with training.

we're not sure it's officially *anorexia nervosa* for the classic psychological reasons, haven't you heard of young wrestlers who starve themselves to reach a certain weight class, or female gymnasts who diet to stave off puberty?

If you think your child has anorexia and/or bulimia, CALL YOUR DOCTOR TODAY. These are serious medical conditions that can and do result in death.

Do everything in your power to help your child avoid eating disorders by helping him understand that his genetic makeup strongly influences his growth, lean-to-fat ratio, weight, and height. Do not permit him to base his self-esteem on a foundation as flimsy as physical appearance. And finally, encourage your child to eat right and exercise to be the best he can be within his genetic destiny.

Chapter 7

Training and Injuries

IF YOUR CHILD IS GOING TO PLAY A SPORT, his body must be ready to meet its demands. In the chapter on nutrition, we already covered a portion of what's necessary to prepare him. Now let's talk about his need for physical training.

Training is exercise that builds your player's strength, endurance, mobility, and speed. Among younger players, or older ones playing recreational sports, training is usually focused on general fitness: building wind; having the endurance to play the game; good eye-hand coordination. At more advanced levels of play, training may involve not only being generally fit, but also focusing on specifics like strength or speed. Whatever level your player is at, you must take the need for training seriously. (In fact, we think you should promote training—or what we call good ol' garden-variety physical fitness—even if you have a child who doesn't play or stay with sports.)

Training is different than practice. Training makes certain the body is physically up to the sport. Coach may incorporate aspects of training in practice (calisthenics, running, wind sprints), but practice focuses on developing sport-specific skills, learning to play the game or perform the event, and, when applicable, playing as a team.

Training does more than prepare your player's body to play the game. It can help prevent injuries, make playing more enjoyable, build his self-confidence, and instill in him positive fitness habits that will last a lifetime.

Yes, indeed, training can work wonders. And guess which lucky person gets to be in charge of all that wonder-working?

That's right, SportsMom. Once again, it's you!

We can almost hear you groan: "Isn't that Coach's responsibility? Or the gym teacher's? Why me?"

Because you are the one who's there to see that your child is physically active, day in and day out. You're the one who must see that he carries through on any training recommendations that Coach or teacher provides. It's also your job to yell, "It's a beautiful day out there! Turn off that TV and get outside and play!"

When it comes to training, you can't expect your kid to go from couch potato to athlete overnight. Nor should you allow your child to think that fitness is something he "does" sometimes, and doesn't do others. He may reduce the intensity of activity in the off-season, but it should never come to a screeching halt.

For the most part, keeping fit should be fun. In fact, before TV and computers turned lots of kids into sedentary little couch spuds, fitness was often a byproduct of having fun: riding bikes, running, skating. Of course, as your child gets more involved in his sport, aspects of advanced training may not be fun (think laps), but overall, he should regard regular physical activity as an enjoyable part of life.

Questions SportsMom Should Ask

Whether your child is involved in garden-variety fitness training or more advanced directives from Coach, you should look at what your child is doing, then ask some important questions:

- Is the training activity safe?
- Does it have a purpose—and what is it?
- If someone other than you has prescribed the regimen, is there a plan? Does the regimen include warm-ups, cardiac conditioning, and exercises to develop strength, flexibility, or eye-hand coordination? Is there a cool-down period?
- Is your child pushing (or being pushed) beyond his abilities and strengths?
- Is there a logical progression in training, or is your child being asked to skip ahead to more advanced levels before he's mastered simpler ones?
- Does training involve a variety of activities to keep your child interested?
- Does the training seem age-appropriate?

What about Weight Training?

That last item brings us to the subject of *weight training,* also known as *strength training.* Its purpose is to increase the strength of specific muscle groups by using weights in exercise. Increasingly, the question among SportsMoms seems to be *Is weight training appropriate for young athletes?*

The answer depends on *how* young.

Weight training is absolutely not appropriate for kids ten and under. The minimal benefit they might gain is far outweighed by the possibility they'll injure themselves. They don't have the judgment to know when the weight is too much; they may even mistake the strain as a good thing. Besides, kids this age can't keep track of their gym bags, let alone a set of weights.

If your child is over age ten, weight training may be appropriate, but proceed with a big SportsMom Caution. If Coach recommends it, check with your child's pediatrician before you give your okay. If weight training is your idea, talk with the doctor and Coach first.

If you decide to proceed, all weight-training sessions must be supervised by an adult who knows what he's doing. You can probably find an experienced trainer at the Y, local sports medicine facility, or health club. If you can't, keep looking, because this is no place for the do-it-yourselfer.

There should be a plan and a purpose to weight training, and it should never be confused with weight *lifting.* They are two very different activities, and you must make certain your child knows that. However, given that kids are kids, you can't count on them to remember that: another very good reason to make certain your young athlete is never left alone to handle this type of training on his own. (You can almost hear their little voices, can't you? *Okay, now let's see who can lift the most. AAAGGGHHH!!!* Helloooo, Mr. Hernia!)

Seriously, unsupervised weight training, or weight training before a child's body is ready to handle it can cause major problems. And so, we'd like to offer *resistance training* as an alternative. It's a much better fit for young athletes.

Unlike weight training, resistance training uses the body's own weight to strengthen muscles. The secret lies in the number of repetitions, not added weights. Abdominal crunches, sit-ups, leg lifts, and push-up are good examples of resistance training.

However, even this "safer" alternative to weight training can have its downside. Too many reps using one joint can result in an overuse injury. That's why resistance training must also be supervised and planned: in a correctly-structured program, different groups of muscles are worked alternately, which gives them a chance to recover. (This is sometimes called *circuit training*.) If you think your child's overdoing the repetitions, point out that too much of a good thing is just that: his joints must last a lifetime, so he'd better start watching out for them now.

Concerning Anabolic Steroids and Other Forms of Stupidity

Anabolic steroids are drugs that some athletes use to enhance their performance by building muscle and providing energy. They should not be confused with the steroid known as corticosteroid, or cortisone, a prescription drug physicians use to treat inflammation.

If you are a fan of the Olympics, you probably know about anabolic steroids and their controversial use by top athletes. What may surprise you is that research indicates that your child probably knows about them, too. In fact, 2.7 percent of child athletes have actually used them.

Speaking as SportsMoms, we think this is pretty scary. Anabolic steroids can have some serious and long-lasting side effects: altering liver function, suppressing growth in children, causing personality changes, and negatively impacting the reproductive system so that you may never have grandchildren, if you get our drift. Steroids can build muscles so big that young ligaments can't hold up to the strain, and *Voila! One blown knee, coming right up.*

We are firmly opposed to the use of anabolic steroids by any athlete at any age. There are some people who will tell you that they're okay as long as your athlete is in puberty or beyond and under the care of a healthcare professional well-versed in the drug and its side effects. To that, we say, "It's not okay with me, Mister," and that's what we recommend that you say, too, should anyone, no matter how well-intentioned, suggest your child use them. We feel the same way about readily-available nutritional supplements used to build muscles. These include dehyroepinadosterone (DHEA), creatine, and androstenedione.

So what if you've said no to such items, but you think your child is taking them on the sly? How can you tell?

Well, first, you're going to notice some pretty impressive bulking up that happens fairly fast. (Think of that actor who used to literally burst out of his clothing as he became the Incredible Hulk.) Look for those personality changes we already mentioned. There are medical tests you can ask your doctor to order, too.

Whatever you do, don't ignore the problem if you think it already exists. If it doesn't, make certain you talk to your child ASAP about the dangers of using anabolic steroids and supplements to enhance performance. This is just as important as talking to him about the dangers of drugs like marijuana and cocaine.

Remind him that the late Lyle Alzado, an NFL All-Pro defensive end, blamed his terminal cancer on steroid use. Point out that as terrific as Mark McGwire's 70-homerun season may have been, there will always be those who consider it diminished by his admitted use of androstenedione to bulk up.

Above all, know what your child is taking. Do not figuratively swallow anything you do not understand, and certainly do not let your children do so literally. The tragic consequences, no matter how unintended, can last your child's lifetime.

Injuries and Expectations

Earlier in this chapter, we said that training can help prevent injuries, and that's certainly true. A player who is strong and coordinated will be less prone to getting hurt than one who's not.

However, even well-conditioned players experience falls and collisions that result in injury. Increasingly, overuse injuries and conditions such as Osgood-Schlatter disease and chondromalacia* are showing up in young athletes. This is particularly troubling, because injuries like these can have a lifelong impact.

From personal experience, we know that injuries are a reality most SportsMoms would prefer didn't exist. In fact, in talking with fellow SportsMoms, especially rookies, we've discovered that most do not expect their children to suffer any short-term injury or develop any long-term physical problems as a result of playing a game. They particularly expect these things will not happen as a result of Coach's poor supervision or lax discipline, or during practices.

We understand this expectation because we, too, don't want to see our kids hurt. However, parts of it are totally unrealistic, so let's examine it, bit by bit.

No short-term injury? Not ever? Get real, SportsMom. Kids fall, they stumble, they run into each other, they skin their knees, they even break bones. While we do think it's reasonable to expect these injuries won't result from poor supervision or lax discipline, it's pretty unreasonable to think your kid is never going to suffer a short-term injury playing

---

* Osgood-Schlatter Disease occurs when a sudden growth in height pulls the tendons that attach the femur (thigh bone) to the tibia and fibula (shin bones). When the tendons are pulled, they become irritated, and the soft tissues surrounding the knee become inflamed. Osgood-Schlatter always follows a growth spurt, is common in physically-active children, and in athletes who run and jump. Chondromalacia occurs when the cartilage that cushions the kneecap is thinned out or has an abnormality on its surface, causing the kneecap to ride directly on the other bones. Lack of the cartilage cushion causes knee pain. Chondromalacia is common in soccer players, skaters, skiers, and bicyclists. It can be caused by poor muscle alignment, muscle weakness, overuse, or be the result of a specific injury.

sports. It doesn't mean you have to like it, but you'd better expect it.

What about no long-term physical problems? These two SportsMoms consider this a reasonable expectation, with a big *but* attached.

Before you give your permission for your child to play a sport, call his pediatrician, a sports medicine doctor, and/or the local physical therapy clinic. Find out which sport's players they see most for injuries, particularly those injuries—like overuse injuries in joints—that have life-long consequences. Whether or not you eliminate a sport with more injury potential is up to you; you may still allow your child to play it, but insist he condition his body in a way that minimizes the risk of injury.

What we're saying here is that you need to be realistic about the possibility of long-term physical problems. If your kid swims, a knee injury should be a surprise. If he plays football, it shouldn't. Some sports simply have higher injury rates, and when you permit your child to play them, you have to accept that—then do everything in your power to prevent them from happening.

Your Role in Preventing Injuries

In addition to the obvious need to make certain your child's coach runs a supervised, well-disciplined practice and game, you can take some steps to help your child avoid injury.

As we've already said, insist that he maintain a baseline level of physical fitness, in season and out. Make certain he complies with any additional training recommendations made by Coach. Monitor what he's doing to make sure he's not in danger of joint overuse.

Then, see that his body has time to rest and recover. This is particularly important for younger athletes who devote themselves to sport: as they sprint from baseball to cross-country to hockey season, their joints and muscles don't get the recovery period they need. That may require you to talk to Coach about pacing practice from every night to alternate days. You may want to consider making your child take time off before starting the next season, or even eliminating a sport.

You also need to observe your child for signs of injury as he plays and practices. Is he favoring one leg because the other hurts? Is he cradling one arm or the other? Can you see pain written on his face? The signs may be even subtler, but that's where all that quantity time you've spent with him pays off: you can read him like a book.

Even if your child is young, don't dismiss the possibility that he'll try to play when he's hurt. Silly as it seems to us, *playing with pain* is viewed positively in our culture. Athletes are expected to grit their teeth and persevere against all odds, and your child may have already picked up on that.

On the other hand, don't dismiss the possibility that your child is feigning injury in order to get out of a situation he doesn't want to be in. At its simplest, this can mean your player "feels bad" when the team has to run its pre-practice mile, then experiences a miraculous recovery when it's time for the scrimmage. Handling that scenario takes the same set of skills you've developed to handle his "life-threatening" stomachache the morning of a big test at school.

More seriously, feigning injury may mean he wants to quit his sport, but he hasn't quite worked up the courage to tell you because he's afraid of disappointing you. Or, he wants out, not because he hates the sport, but he's afraid he won't make the grade. If you have the slightest inkling that either of these is the case, give your child an opening to talk about it. You may want to mention that sometimes our bodies have a funny way of getting us out of situations we do not want to be in. You may talk about a time you feared failure and didn't know what to do. Above all, let him know that whatever he's feeling, it's okay to tell you.

SportsMom Mouths Off on Equipment

Preventing injury is also about having the right equipment protecting the right body part. You'll no doubt be briefed by Coach on what your child needs for his sport, but if you aren't, or if you have questions or concerns, speak up *before* your child steps foot on the field/rink/floor.

One piece of equipment that may not be required in your child's sport, but which we *strongly* recommend, is a mouthpiece. Some sports, like hockey, require them, while others, like basketball, don't. Frankly, that is a mystery to us. We figure that if elbows are flying and your kid's mouth could hit a hard surface—be it ice or hardwood floor—there's a chance he could lose teeth.

If Your Child is Injured

The time to think about what you should do if your child is injured during practice or a competition is now, before it happens.

Usually, Coach is the front line when an injury takes place. He should take charge, and you should remain calm, and follow his cues. Nothing will embarrass your child more than your storming the field, demanding to see what's wrong.

However, if you believe that your child's injury will be made worse because it's apparent that no one knows what he's doing, you must step in.

First, do not get weepy, panicky, or hysterical. There'll be plenty of time to do all those things once the situation is handled, your child is safe, and you're someplace private where you can give way to your emotions. Right now, your child needs you to be The Rock. You may be Jell-O® inside, but he must not know it.

Take over just as you would at home if your child fell off a swing set on his head, or took a line drive to the chin off his sister's bat. Get a sense of what the injury is about, call in medical professionals (*aka* ambulance) if you need to, and stay with your child. Ask another SportsMom to watch over your other kids on the sidelines, call your spouse for you, or even babysit for a few hours if you need to head for the hospital.

If the injury does not require medical attention, or your child is experiencing minor soreness, follow the RICE rule:

- **Rest** the sore joint or muscle.
- Apply **Ice.** Ice can range from ready-made sports ice packs to ice with a little cold water in a plastic bag to—our favorite—a bag of frozen peas. Whichever form you prefer, wrap it in a thin towel or t-shirt and place it on the injured area for no more than 20 minutes on, 40 minutes off an hour. Do not place ice directly on the skin.

- **Compress** the area by wrapping it with an Ace® bandage (but not too tight).
- Then **Elevate** it. A dose of ibuprofen (Motrin®, Advil®) will help reduce swelling and ease the pain.

Keep in mind that the RICE rule applies only to minor injuries and soreness. If you're not sure it's minor, or if it's minor, but seems to be lingering on and on, follow the SportsMom Rule on Injuries: *When in doubt, call the doctor.* Chances are, a chat with the office nurse will tell you if your child's condition requires further attention.

PART THREE

And Now We're Ready To Play

Chapter 8

Coach and You

FINALLY. AT LAST. ABOUT TIME.

After all the preparation, your child is about to actually participate in his beloved sport. Or is he?

That depends on what Coach says. And therein lies an important principle you must keep in mind throughout your child's organized sports experience.

This Is Coach's Show

Always remember that Coach is in charge, and you are not. It's his role to lead, to set the tone, and to make decisions. If Coach prescribes a training program or diet regimen for your child, yours is not to reason why (unless we're talking something truly dangerous). Yours is to "just do it," to borrow a phrase from the sports shoe people.

You may be asking yourself, "So who died and made Coach God?" *You* did, SportsMom. By virtue of signing your child up to participate, you authorized Coach to be, well, Coach.

Bottom line, this is his show. In theory, that's easy to accept, but in reality it's sometimes tough to handle.

You may think your child should play or perform, but Coach doesn't. (We'll cover the issue of playing time a bit later). Or Coach demands you have your kid at the playing field forty-five minutes before game time, but you've got a zillion errands to run, another child who needs to be across town, and laundry to catch up on. It seems stupid to stand around for nearly an hour before the game begins, doesn't it?

Well, maybe. But if that's what Coach says, that's what you do. When it comes to the team, he's the center of the universe, and you, just a planet in his orbit. He rules, and you don't. When you bought into the sport, you bought into Coach. If you're not prepared to do the latter, don't do the former.

We would never claim that following Coach's edicts is always easy. However, you are actually doing yourself one huge favor when you do: you are teaching your child how to live with authority. And, since you are the major authority in your child's life, you are, by example, showing him how to respond to you.

If You Disagree with Coach

Accepting Coach's authority over the team does not mean giving up your right to disagree with him. However, it's vital that you handle your differences in a way that still shows Coach the respect he deserves.

Let's go back to that 45-minute-before-game issue. Since Coach requires it, you have to do it, even though you think it's stupid. What you must not do is express your opinion that it's stupid to your child, even if he thinks it is, too. You can sympathize and agree that it's tough to get there that early, but you cannot imply or say that Coach is a twit for demanding it. If you do the latter, you are showing disrespect for Coach as a person. You are also teaching your child, by example, precisely how to demonstrate disrespect to you.

What if you disagree with Coach on something more serious? We suggest you go talk to him privately, without your child or other parents and kids around. Whether or not you let your child know you are concerned about the issue or talked to Coach is totally up to you. However, if you do, remember to express it in a way that demonstrates respect. It's not, "How insensitive can that man be to schedule practice every Sunday at 10:30 a.m.? Doesn't he know that some people go to church? I'm going to give him a piece of my mind." Instead, it's "I plan to talk to Coach about the conflict between church and Sunday morning practices and see if we can work something out."

It may be tough to do, particularly if you're angry, but you'll be providing your child with a model of how people can handle their differences while maintaining respect for each other.

"But what if I don't respect Coach?" you ask.

Then respect his *position* as Coach, and teach your child to do the same. You and your child signed up for this gig of your own free will. It may not be playing out precisely the way you thought it should, but you have an obligation to help your child learn how to fulfill a commitment when things don't go well. You'll be preparing him to handle a great many life circumstances if you do.

Of course, if Coach does something that actually puts your child in physical or psychological danger, you should step in immediately, protect your child, and report Coach to the league, association, or other governing body. Chances are, however, that you'll never be faced with this situation: it's our observation that stereotypical, win-at-all-costs, abusive coaches portrayed in movies like *The Mighty Ducks* are few and far between in real life.

Keeping the Lines of Communication Open

When we were Rookie SportsMoms, we assumed that, since Coach was in charge, it was his responsibility to bring us into the loop and keep us there via his clear, consistent communication. We've since discovered that most new SportsMoms expect the same thing.

However, experience has taught us that the quality and consistency of communication varies considerably from coach to coach. Some limit themselves to the basics: an initial meeting that covers such details as practice and game times, team rules, and the cost of uniforms. On the other extreme are coaches who publish regular newsletters and hand out booklets that cover everything from philosophy to training tips.

Unless your coach is a master communicator, you must take the initiative on communication. If you need information, ask Coach politely. If you have a complaint, go to Coach directly, and encourage other parents to do the same. Do not gossip about Coach, do not complain about him to other parents, and do not allow yourself to be drawn into the complaining conversations of other parents.

Remember that Coach is human, and, therefore, not perfect. He may not always handle every situation smoothly. But hey—do you? So cut him some slack, SportsMom, and you may find he returns the favor.

Above all, keep the lines of communication with Coach open. Deal with him fairly, directly, and honestly. And always remember that you're both on the same side.

To Play, or Not to Play: That is the Question

We haven't conducted a scientific survey to determine the Number One Complaint SportsMoms have about Coach,

but we think we're safe in saying it's the issue of playing time, as in *My child's not getting enough.* (There may be a SportsMom somewhere who complains that her child plays too much, but we've yet to meet her.)

If you're concerned about how little time your

child is playing, we understand where you're coming from. By the time you've gone through all the rigamarole involved in getting your child ready to compete, it seems reasonable to expect that Coach will give your child the opportunity to reach his goals by letting him play. You figure that if equal fees have been paid, equal practices were attended, and equal fund raising required, then playing time ought to be equal, too. (Although we're using team sport terms here, the playing time issue has an equivalent in individual sports: being ranked in some type of pecking order, such as seeds in tennis, flights in ice skating, or levels in gymnastics.)

You've heard the arguments, and maybe even made a few of them yourself: *My kid spent as much time as the other players collecting donations, so why isn't he getting equal playing time (or ranking)? How can he learn all these wonderful lessons sports are supposed to teach if he never gets any playing time?*

So what's our SportsMom take on this subject? A firm, definite *it depends.*

When players are young and in the early stages of sports development, we think there's a good argument for equal playing time. However, when kids begin to grow in their sport, and/or as they mature, there's an equally good reason for increased playing time based on ability.

The reason? Because that's how life works.

Life is competitive, and success (a real-life equivalent of playing time) is predicated, in large measure, on ability. Expecting equal time for all players at intermediate and upper levels of the game does service to no one. We're not advocating that players with lesser abilities be barred from earning more time as their game matures, nor are we saying that you cannot rationally discuss your concerns about playing time with Coach and ask for his perspective. We are suggesting that you take a good look at what Valuable Lessons of Life your child can learn as playing time begins to be doled out increasingly on the basis of ability.

Remember: no one said that *playing time* would teach him lessons; they said *sports* would. For some players, sports means being the star: in that case your job is to help your child learn to handle stardom with grace, humility, and appreciation for the other players who support him. For other players, sports means sitting the bench more than they'd like: in that case your job is to emphasize the importance of your player's supporting role, then point out other areas in which your child excels.

It's your responsibility to help your player learn Important Lessons of Life from his sport, no matter the time he spends playing. So take a deep breath, step back for a minute, and focus on what it was you were trying to accomplish in your child's life by letting him participate in sports.

What you help him learn through this experience will prepare him for future real-life challenges on the job. Let's say that someday he's passed over for a promotion because someone else is better qualified. Which present-day scenario will better prepare him to handle it? Your demanding that Coach put him in because it's "not fair," or your helping your child evaluate the situation (perhaps even with Coach's input), see where he might improve, and/or appreciate the contribution he does make?

We realize that, despite our argument, there may still be those among you who think your child deserves equal time at intermediate or advanced levels of play, despite his skill level. That's your privilege.

However, by now you may have noticed that we rarely make a strong argument like this unless we're truly convinced of the seriousness of the issue: for example, we've taken a strong stand against anabolic steroids. If that isn't enough to convince you, there's a very practical issue we raised in an earlier chapter: if you make a big enough pain of yourself over playing time, Coach may be reluctant to have your child on his team next year, and the grapevine for coaches is pretty strong, too.

Sports don't last forever, but the values you teach him through sports will remain with him throughout his life, SportsMom. Please, just keep that in mind.

Coach as a Positive Role Model

So far in this chapter, we've focused on your responsibility to maintain a line of communication with Coach. But there's one area of "communication" that lies squarely on Coach's shoulders: communicating to your child, by example, positive behavior.

Face it: your child may have wanted to participate in a sport because he loved it or wanted to be with his buddies, but you had ulterior motives. You figured sports would provide an alternative to his growing up too quickly, as well as preventing his involvement in sex, drugs, and rock 'n' roll.*

By devoting time to his sport, your child automatically reduces the amount of empty time he has to fill. As SportsMom, that's what you're looking for, because too much

---

* We are not referring to rock 'n' roll in the literal sense. In our day, the phrase *sex, drugs, and rock 'n roll* was used by irate parents to describe the general evils tempting their teens.

time and too little to do can add up to big trouble. In fact, keeping your kid busy is one of sports' biggest benefits.

And so you've invested a considerable amount of time and money in the youth sports experience. We think there are certain things you should expect that Coach will do to support your efforts to keep your kids out of trouble.

It's reasonable to expect Coach to be a positive role model. He shouldn't wear t-shirts to practice that have sexual connotations, or advertise alcohol or tobacco. He shouldn't break open a beer after practice is over.

A good coach should encourage your player to make academics his top priority. He should discourage disrespectful attitudes and inappropriate language. Those are all quite reasonable expectations, and fair game for discussion with Coach if he's failing to meet them.

However—and it seems we always get back to this—the primary responsibility for keeping your kid out of trouble and making sure he stays a kid as long as possible rests with you. Sports can keep your kid occupied, and Coach can reinforce positive behavior by acting as a good role model for your child. However, neither is a substitute for parental guidance and involvement.

SportsMom™

© 1998 KBL

BOB'S NEW CARS

"It's o.k., Mom, I only spilled a little and it's mostly on the seat."

C h a p t e r   9

What You Should Expect from Your Child (and What Your Child Should Expect from You)

By THE TIME YOUR CHILD actually gets to compete, you are aware—if you weren't before—that youth sports is not just something *he* does: you're in this together. Anytime two people share an experience, each has expectations of what the other guy ought to be doing.

So what should you and your child expect of each other as you wend your way down the Path of Youth Sports?

Hold Him to His Promises—and Keep Yours, Too

As SportsMom, you should expect your child to honor the commitment he made to his sport. That means keeping all those promises he made up front: *I'll keep my grades up. I won't complain about practices. I'll do extra chores to help you since you have to drive me to games. I won't ask for the new computer game because I know my sport is costing a lot of money.*

Remember earlier, when we told you to write down these undying pledges and keep the list handy? You'll need to pull it out from time to time to keep him on the straight and narrow.

It's reasonable for your child to expect that you'll keep up your end of the deal, too. We've already touched on much of this: follow Coach's instructions, deliver your player to practices and games on time, don't decide halfway through the season that this gig has got to go.

> It's your responsibility to use sports as a vehicle to help your child develop and grow as a person.

It's also reasonable for your child to expect that you'll practice what you preach, or that you'll "model behavior," as experts in child development term it. If you want him to respect Coach, then you must, too. If you want your player to display good sportsmanship, you can't be cussing out the ref. In other words, your child has every right to expect you to set a good example.

However, there is one more thing your child should expect of you—whether he knows to or not. He should expect that, throughout this entire sports experience, you, as his parent, will look out for his best interests as a human being, not just as an athlete. This is another way of saying what we've stressed throughout this book: that it's your responsibility to use sports as a vehicle to help your child develop and grow as a person. If he becomes a great athlete in the process, that's terrific, but it's secondary to his becoming a great human being.

Build His Confidence

One of the most important things you can do to help your child navigate his way through life successfully is to build his self-confidence.

It's our observation that some kids are born with more confidence than others. But no matter how much your child was gifted with at birth, you can use the sports experience to help him build upon it.

In great part, a child's self-confidence is based on his parent's confidence in him. When he sees that you believe in him, he believes in himself. This is especially true when a child is young. (Enjoy this period of your child's life: all too soon his peers' opinions will take precedence over yours.) As you continue to express your confidence in what he does, he begins to build his own reservoir of belief in himself. Eventually, he can draw on that for self-affirmation.

Although we're discussing sports and affirmation, we don't believe that SportsMom's main focus ought to be on affirming sports skills. Instead, we think it's more important to let your child know that you like him and what he is doing by taking part in the sport. You appreciate the work it takes to participate. You recognize and respect him for the risk he's taking by performing out there in front of everybody, where he just might make a mistake. You like the fact that he tries his best, even though he routinely spends the second half on the bench. You particularly appreciate that he cheers for his teammates instead of moping because he isn't playing. Or, if he's the star, you're pleased that he high-fives his teammates when he scores a goal, rather than bragging about how terrific he is.

When it comes to building your kid's self-confidence, your word does count. So affirm behavior you like and praise him when he reacts positively in negative situations. There's more to be learned by handling one bad situation well than by experiencing ten that go off without a hitch.

If your child fails in some way, do not lie. If he strikes out at bat or falls on the ice, you can't say it's a good thing without endangering your credibility. You can say he handled the situation well (if he did); if he didn't, tell him, say you have confidence he'll do better in the future, then offer suggestions as to how he might.

Even when you know in your heart of hearts that it was your child's fault that he blew it, you may so desperately want to soften the sting of defeat that you're tempted to make excuses or blame others. Don't do it, SportsMom! Don't lash out at Coach, or the ref, or the dirty players on the other team. Don't say the rink was too small or the winds were too fierce or the planets weren't lined up right. Instead, use the opportunity to help your child learn how to handle defeat gracefully, look for ways to improve, and build confidence and character in the process.

If your child is young, and defeat gives rise to tears, don't listen to those folks who say he shouldn't cry, that he shouldn't be "such a baby." If he were in college we would agree (national championship or Olympic losses excepted), but right now he's a little kid with shaken confidence who needs his SportsMom: when you see that lip quivering, rescue him, and protect him so others don't see his embarrassment. This is different than encouraging a child who always uses tears or pouting to get his way.

As your child becomes a teen, he still needs your affirmation, but he'll undoubtedly be too busy being overconfident (in that truly annoying way adolescents have) to recognize it. In fact, he may be embarrassed if you openly express your belief in him. He would be mortified if you even noticed his eyes welling up in the face of a major defeat.

What you should do instead is listen. When his confidence is flagging, when he's lost that directional rudder momentarily, tune in to what he's saying. Make sympathetic noises. Ask leading questions. If invited, throw in your two cents' worth. If not invited, bide your time, go back to the subject later when your teen's emotion has been diffused, and provide him with a reality check.

Remember when your mom used to say, "It's not what you say, but how you say it?" Well, when it comes to building your child's self-confidence through sports, it's not what happens, but how your child interprets what happens. Your

SportsMom™

"What do you mean, did I pack your shinguards?!"

job is to teach him to interpret his experiences in a way that increases healthy self-confidence.

Building your child's confidence as a person does not preclude building his confidence as an athlete. If he makes a good play or improves his skills, be sure to compliment him. Just make certain that your primary focus is developing his confidence and character as a human being, because athletics eventually end, but life goes on.

Help Him Learn Important Lessons of Life

Throughout this book, we've talked about using the sports experience to teach your child important Lessons of Life. These lessons are varied, and the opportunities to impart them can arise anytime, so it's best to be prepared.

First, recognize that most, if not all, of these Life Lessons are learned through difficult situations, not easy ones. When Sports Life is Good, your child simply enjoys it. When Sports Life is Bad, he learns—or at least he has the opportunity to do so if you frame the experience correctly. It's those tough times that can teach Lessons of Life, so don't totally despair when something bad happens: there is a silver lining in that cloud, if you just poke around a little bit to find it.

In this section, we'll list some of the more common complaints kids make, point out the lessons we think are to be learned from them, and offer suggestions on how to handle them, based on experience with our athletes.

Your player, your situation, and your values may differ from ours, so you may not agree with everything we say here. That's okay, because he is your child and you know the Life Lessons you want him to take away from the sports experience. Our goal is not to have you accept what we say as gospel, but to use it as a springboard to start thinking about how you will handle these and other issues if they arise.

(Note: We're presenting these problems as if your child were verbalizing them, but he's just as likely to express complaints through actions or body language.)

Your Child Says:
I want to be on a better team, Mom.

Lessons of Life:
The value of hard work, personal responsibility, following through on commitments

If you're dealing with a child whose skills far outstrip his teammates', a player who really should be on a better team, he must learn that his current commitment to his team takes precedence over his personal desire to move on. In the process of sticking it out, he can learn patience and improve his individual skill level.

If ego is raising its ugly head, he must learn humility, and/or that athletic ability does not entitle him to special privileges. You may need to help him realize that he must respect his teammates as human beings, regardless of their skill level.

What if your child wants to be on a winning team because he thinks his current teammates are all losers who are holding him back, when, in fact, his skills are no better than theirs? Then you must teach him not to blame others for the situation he's in. Help him honestly assess his own skills, then see that his abilities are in part responsible for the fact the team isn't winning. Make it clear that if he wants to be on a better team, it's up to him to improve enough to help make it better.

If your child has average skills and voices this complaint, you need to discover the reason behind it. Is he tired of losing, or does he want the experience of being on a winning team? Then stress the positives of the team he's on, and fall back on that old adage, "It's not whether you win or lose, but how you play the game." (Adages usually become old because they're true.) Not every experience in life is a winning one, and he'd better learn to handle reality now. See what you can do to inject more fun in the sports experience, be it a pool party or group outing to—dare we say it?—Chuck E. Cheese™ or Putt-Putt™.

No matter why your child voices his desire to compete at a higher level, consider if he's doing so because he doesn't want to disappoint you, or because he's picked up on the cultural emphasis on winning. If either is the case, reassure him that doing his best is much more important than actually winning.

Your Child Says:
I don't like Coach, Mom.
Lessons of Life:
Dealing with authority, respecting others, compromise

Your first job, SportsMom, is to find out why.

If Coach is a likable guy, but he made an unpopular decision, or required extra laps at practice, or is pushing your child to play to his potential, then talk to your child about learning to separate what a person does from who that person is. Also address whether or not your child's not liking Coach's action is reasonable, or based on selfishness or laziness.

What if Coach is not terribly likable and made a decision you don't agree with but which is not actually harmful? Again, talk to your child about separating the person from the decision, but add this twist: focus on the need to respect Coach's position. Your child must understand that he may not always like Coach or his decisions, but he must respect his authority as head of the team.

Your Child Says:

My teammates "hate" me, or I "hate" my teammates.

Lessons of Life:

Getting along with others, learning that your actions have consequences

Every SportsMom wants her child to be liked, but it doesn't always happen.

If your child thinks his teammates hate him, ask him why. Is it because he's shy, so they think he's stuck up? Is he new to a team where friendships are already established, so he's odd man out? Are his teammates just a bunch of heartless bullies who victimize the more sensitive among them? Or—and no SportsMom likes to face this—is your child acting in a way that makes him unlikable? Is he a braggart, a bully, or a whiner who blames others for his mistakes?

If he's shy or new, encourage him to invite some kids to go for pizza, or you might offer to drive a bunch of kids to the next game. If his teammates are cruel, but there's no physical abuse involved, teach him about rising above it all, then think about whether or not he should switch teams once his current commitment is up. If he's getting beat up or the psychological abuse is extreme, talk to Coach ASAP: he should be aware of what's going on and put a stop to it.

However, if your child is not liked because he's the problem, your job is to help him see that he is reaping what he sowed. Find out why he's being that way. Suggest ways he can change. Tell him that when he chooses to indulge in obnoxious behavior, he also chooses to go friendless. Do not let him blame others if the problem is his.

Your Child Says:
I don't want to practice, Mom.

Lessons of Life:
Self-discipline, perseverance, resilience, commitment

Unless your child is that rare exception who loves practicing, you're bound to hear this more than once. Your athlete may know he needs to practice, but it's a drag sometimes, and—since he rarely opts to suffer in silence—you hear about it.

Don't try to deny that practice can be the pits: there are times when it is. Instead, remind him that practice translates to becoming a skilled athlete and a high-performance team, as well as to creative play during competitions. When any or all of these things finally happens, be sure to relate it to his perseverance in practice. In doing so, you'll help him recognize that sticking with an endeavor—even when it's boring—does pay off in the long run.

You may want to underscore the importance of practice by showing up for a few (unless he's at the stage where your presence will cause near-fatal embarrassment). When he sticks with practice, reward his self-discipline with those new shoes he wants, or with a special privilege or outing. Be sure to tell him you're proud of him.

Your Child Says:
I'm afraid I'll mess up.
Lesson of Life:
If you don't make mistakes, you don't learn.

We think that sometimes we SportsMoms don't fully appreciate the risks our children take when they participate in sports.

As we mentioned before, your child is performing out there in front of everybody, so the prospect of making a mistake is pretty scary. You can't lessen the risk, but you can help your child understand that making mistakes is part of life. Point out that we all learn by making mistakes.

Then, help your player train his mind to mentally handle the pressure he's feeling. He already knows he must train his body to physically perform. If he practices developing a proper mindset, it will automatically shift into gear during times of stress, just as his body kicks into automatic when the pressure is on.

There are several mental "calisthenics" you should teach your athlete to help him do this. First, talk to him about not dwelling on things that can't be controlled. Help him focus on what he does right when he performs so he begins to trust himself and his abilities. Remind him that he knows his stuff, and should deliver it just like he practiced it. Tell him that if negative thoughts pop up when the pressure's on, he should picture a door, put those thoughts behind it, and mentally turn the key. He can open the door at another time when he can then turn those negative thoughts into a positive strategy.

Explain that the butterflies he feels prior to a game or performance are a good thing: his body's way of signaling his mind to get in gear. Finally, set a tone of calm confidence for your child, even if you, too, are nervous about how he'll do. He'll take his cue from you, so make it the right one.

Your Child Says:
I can't get everything done, Mom.
Lessons of Life:
Time management, establishing priorities, compromise

Take a close look at this one, SportsMom.

Is your child overwhelmed temporarily by the unfortunate confluence of a tournament, science fair project, and big test in math? Is "overwhelmed" a perpetual state of affairs? Or is he overwhelmed because he's a perfectionist? ("I should be so lucky," some of you are muttering at that query.)

If this is a temporary state of affairs—well, it won't be the last clutch situation he faces in life, so this is a good time to help him learn how to cope. There are plenty of lessons to be learned: organization, setting priorities, staying focused, deferring pleasure to fulfill obligations.

However, if your child is always overwhelmed, you've got a couple things to consider. Does he need better management skills, along the lines of those we just mentioned? Is he actually involved in more activities than he can handle? (How many is too many depends on the child.) Or does he hold himself to standards that are impossible to meet?

Overbooking kids wasn't such a problem a generation or two ago. Today, it seems that every kid takes lessons, plays a sport, and is generally scheduled to the max. All this may just be too much for your child, physically and/or psychologically. Talk with your child about this. Then, if you agree that he's involved in too much at the moment, develop a plan to reduce his activity while still maintaining his commitments. That may mean he must continue at the same high level of activity until he's met his obligations, but knowing it will ease off eventually will probably make him feel better. You may even want to temporarily relieve him of some household responsibilities to reduce the pressure.

If he's having difficulty because he's a perfectionist, help him understand that it's important to set priorities in life: not every task merits perfection. Assure him that your good opinion of him rests, not on what he does, but who he is. Then, ask yourself if he's picking up nonverbal clues from you: are your standards for yourself too high? Are you frustrated and angry when something you're doing falls short of perfection? Do you tell him he need not do everything perfectly, but then praise him to the skies when he does—a lot more than when he doesn't?

No matter the reason your child feels overwhelmed, take him seriously. And don't necessarily wait till he verbalizes the problem: keep your eyes open for signs that he's in over his head. Is he always tense, irritable, tired, withdrawn, or cynical? Does he have trouble sleeping? Is there sufficient time between sports seasons for his young body to rest and recuperate? Does he have enough time to simply be a kid?

It's important to teach your child how to handle multiple activities and temporary rushes. It's just as important to teach him that recognizing he's in over his head is not a sign of weakness, but maturity.

Your Child Says:
I don't want to do this anymore, Mom.
Lessons of Life:
Decision-making, knowing when to stay and when to quit, accepting consequences

Many a SportsMom panics when her child wants to quit his sport. As we've said before, you fear that if he gives up on this activity, he'll establish a pattern of bugging out every time the going gets rough, or when the luster of a new endeavor dims.

Talk to your child and find out if the problem is the sport, or if his desire to quit is just a symptom of another problem. Did he say he wanted to quit in a fit of passing frustration, or does he really mean it?

If your child is truly sick and tired of his sport, this is prime time for the Lesson of Life called "How to Make a Mature Decision." You must help your athlete learn the fine line between being a quitter and making a mature decision to quit. Help him see how his reasons for quitting measure up on the maturity scale. Whether his reasons are good or bad, make sure some time passes before you, together, make a final decision about staying on or leaving the sport after the season is over.

If you believe he should stay with his sport, and he disagrees, you might consider giving him some options: *If you still want to quit after next season, you may,* or *You must talk to Coach about your feelings before you make a final decision.*

If you believe that quitting is a mature decision, make certain your player knows that he must still fulfill his commitments to the team and/or Coach. He must also find another activity to keep him physically fit.

Your Child Says:
I don't get enough playing time.
Lessons of Life:
Recognizing and learning to live with and value your abilities; realizing that the dignity is in the worker, not the work

Because this is perhaps the most common concern of players and their SportsMoms, we addressed this problem and the lessons to be learned from it in Chapter 8.

Your Child's Coach Says:
Your child's not playing to his potential, SportsMom.
Lessons of Life:
Setting and living with goals; the value of hard work

When Coach brings this to your attention, find out precisely what he means by it, and what he thinks should be done to remedy the situation. If you notice it yourself, go to Coach and see if he agrees. What you end up doing about it should be based on the goals you and your child established for this sports experience.

If your child is young and/or your goal was that he have fun and learn to get along with others, playing to potential may not be that big a deal to you. If the sport was supposed to be an outlet for your prone-to-perfection, overly-intense child, you may consider the issue of his playing to potential unimportant. It may be more important for a perfectionist child to have an area in which he doesn't feel compelled to excel, even if he has the talent to do so. If any of these scenarios is the case, tell Coach you appreciate his concern, then explain your position.

Not playing to potential is something else altogether if your child wanted to be a great player on a team destined for a championship season. Talk to your child to find out what the problem is. Is he bored? Is this not as much fun as he thought it would be? Is he afraid of failing? Is he lazy? Is his schedule so overloaded that he doesn't have time to improve his skills at home? Does he dislike his teammates? Did the season turn out to be less-than-championship caliber? Is he just not thinking or committed?

Whatever the reason, if working to potential was his goal and he's not meeting it, help him understand the importance of doing so. Help him identify the strengths and talents he can build on. Stress his obligation, not just to others, but to himself. Help him recall how good it felt when he achieved his goals in the past—and how bad it felt when he didn't. Help him map out a strategy for getting back on track. Then, keep an eye on his progress and offer encouragement every step of the way.

Although we've talked in this section about some common problems and their potential for teaching your child important Lessons of Life, there are dozens more you'll no doubt face. When you do, look for the lessons they might teach, and how those lessons relate to your goals for your child's sports experience. (SportsMom Warning: Not every moment of every sports experience must be a lesson. If you try to turn everything into a lesson, your child will automatically tune you out.)

Remember that while youth sports can teach your child, what they teach him is largely up to you. So grab the wheel of this terrific parenting vehicle, then steer it in the direction you want your child to go.

Chapter 10

Getting Along with the Rest of the Cast of Characters

WE'VE ALREADY TALKED ABOUT getting along with Coach, and your relationship with your child during the organized sports experience.

Now, let's discuss those other people who will be affected by your child's sport: your other children (if you have them), your significant other (and your relationship therewith), and assorted relatives. Then we'll move on to those folks you're going to come in contact with as a result of your child's sport: other parents and sports officials.

If You Have Other Children—Or If You Don't

You already know that when your child made a commitment to his sport, it made an impact on *your* life. You may not be as aware that it also affected the lives of other members of your family.

That time you used to spend doing things as a family on Saturday mornings is now spent at games. Your littlest one's after school playtime is regularly interrupted because she has to come along to her older sister's practices. Your oldest son feels overburdened because you've asked him to pick up a regular chore for his brother during a particularly busy foot-

ball season. Or, you have several kids involved in sports, none of whom think he's getting "equal time" from you.

How do you handle all this, given that running off to Mexico under an assumed name is not an option?

First, recognize that every SportsMom faces these same problems. They are not the result of mismanagement. They're the result of 1) making changes in a routine your family was comfortable with; 2) each of your children having his own needs and a fervent desire to see them fulfilled; and 3) the unfortunate fact that there are just twenty-four hours in a day.

Talk to your kids about the situation. Stress that people who make up a family help and support each other, and you expect that kind of behavior from them. Compare it to the

SportsMom™

"Not exactly what I had in mind for a weekend getaway..."

way their sports team works. (Keep your notes from this speech: you'll be delivering it more than once.)

However, even if your speech is inspiring and your kids are pretty good about cooperating to make your family's crazy schedule work, there will come a time when at least one of them suggests he is not being treated fairly. He feels you are spending more time focused on his siblings' activities. Your child wants more of your time—and he wants it now.

When this happens—and it will, SportsMom—do not think in terms of time equity. You could produce detailed charts that document that you devoted precisely the same amount of time down to the nanosecond to each of your children's interests (or, in the case of the only child, that you have indeed left work early to attend his competitions, etc.). All may be technically equal, and still not be giving your child what he wants.

So find out what he means by *It's not fair, Mom. You care more about what everyone else is doing than you do about me.*

It could mean that you've been so busy keeping up with his sibling's game schedule that you haven't helped him with homework the way you used to. It might mean that you attended his band concert, but spent too much time talking with other parents after the concert instead of focusing on how great his performance was. Or, it may be his way of telling you that he feels lost in the shuffle of school, homework, household chores, and his sibling's sport.

Help him sort out what he really wants from you. Ask him what he would like to see happen that didn't. (This request usually gives way to thoughtful silence, while you sit there wondering if you just opened Pandora's Box of Shoulda, Coulda, Woulda.) What you end up doing about the situation should be guided by what your child feels he's missing.

If he wants you to see him do his thing every time he does it, it's time for a reality check. Tell him straight up that you can't commit to that, but that you will do your best to be present for those moments he considers most important. Then pull out the family calendar and, together, figure out how to make this happen. When there are conflicts, especially with other children's activities, consider the needs of each child. Which activity does each consider it most important you attend?

Even if you have one child, there's still a need to go through this exercise. In lieu of a brother or sister to blame, an only child will say you're spending more time on work or your own interests than on him.

However, all children must realize that, while they are very important to you, you also have other obligations in your life. If you work outside the home, you may not always be able to take time off to see afternoon competitions: doing so places unfair burdens on your co-workers, or may jeopardize your job. This is a reality your child must learn to accept. You can make it easier by showing great enthusiasm for his detailed play-by-play the evening of the game, by saying you wish you could be at all his events, and by promising to make it to the most important competition of the season.

There are a few other things you must consider when your child starts waving the *It's Not Fair* banner in your face.

First, maybe you aren't being fair. This is tough to admit, but it might be true. Do you focus more attention on the child who plays the sport you played in high school? Do you pay more compliments to the one who's the star than you do to the one who sits the bench? Do you brag to friends and relatives about your baseball player and neglect to mention your young pianist's accomplishments? If yours is an only child, do you always put your golf game ahead of his sport, even when you have an option?

If you see yourself here, take steps to correct the situation. As we've said before—and it bears repeating—what your children want more than anything in the world is your love and attention. One way they measure that is by the amount of time you spend with them, and the interest you express in what's important to them. When they see a sibling or work getting more than they are, they feel unloved.

What if you're being pretty equitable with your kids, but one still levels a charge of unfairness? Have you ever considered that he may be trying to make you feel guilty enough that you cough up extra attention or a special favor?

Don't get us wrong: we love children, but we know that they're not above this kind of manipulation. The irony is that it often works best on SportsMoms who are already knocking themselves out for their kids because they fear they're not doing enough.

Our editor, whose mother had to work full-time back in the days when most other moms stayed home (and all the villainesses in soap operas were working women), says that she routinely played on her mother's tendency to feel guilty about the situation. Then her mom finally caught on. At that point, her mother made it clear that her working was necessary to the Survival of the Family As Team, and our editor better get with the game plan. Her mom was wise enough to know that she had to get a grip on her feelings of guilt, rather than let her daughter indulge in emotional blackmail. If this is what's happening at your house, we suggest you follow her lead.

Your Significant Other

Some SportsMoms are married; others are not, but have what used to be called boyfriends. Still others are navigating life solo, so we won't belabor this section on significant others.

Suffice it to say that if you have a partnership of some kind, and you want it to last, you cannot completely neglect it when sports season begins. Be certain you carve out time just for the two of you, even if it's minimal: we read a study recently that showed that couples who devoted less than 10 minutes a day to real conversation were able to maintain good marriages.

Do this for yourself so you don't look up one day after the kids have left the nest and wonder just who that person is who claims to be your husband or partner. Do it for your kids so they see how adults manage to have meaningful relationships when life gets wild and crazy.

Assorted Relatives

If grandmothers and grandfathers, aunts and uncles, and other assorted members of your extended family live nearby, encourage them to become actively involved in your child's sports experience. It's one more way they can relate to your child and spend time focusing on what's important to him. Getting involved may also head off complaints like "The kids are so busy we never see them anymore." Which brings us to another point about relatives.

Because organized youth sports on a widespread scale are a recent phenomena, you may have to deal with well-meaning (but annoying) advice/statements, particularly from your parents or in-laws: *Why are those kids involved in so much? We didn't do any of that in my time, and you (or your significant other) turned out just fine. This is pure foolishness, all this running around.*

Count to 10 slowly, SportsMom. Keep in mind that they probably do mean well. Paste a smile on your face and tell them how much you appreciate their concern. Explain that yes, this is different than when they raised kids, but it's what's happening now, your child wants to take part in it, and you see definite benefits. Say that you imagine that, based on the times and their particular circumstances, they raised their own children a little differently than their parents raised them. Then end the conversation by changing the subject.

Other Parents

SportsParents are like any other group of people involved in a common activity. There are decision-makers, influencers, and those who choose to stay on the periphery. Some are positive; others whine. You can rely on some and not on others. How each SportsParent fits in the picture depends upon his background, experience, values, and the common ground you share, which is usually the kids.

No matter what the other SportsParents are like, you must learn to work with them. The degree to which you must cooperate usually increases with your child's age and level of play. However, no matter the circumstances, you must go beyond casual sidelines' socializing to establish a working relationship with the other SportsMoms and Dads in your sphere.

The reasons?

First, a good relationship with other parents sets the tone for your child's relationships with his teammates. When your child is young, you can enlist the help of other SportsParents if your child isn't fitting in. Sometimes a gentle nudge in the form of a sleepover or invitation to a birthday party is all it takes to get your child over that hump. (Your involvement is less appropriate as the child grows older: then, he must learn to get over the hump himself.)

Second, by demonstrating your desire to cooperate with other parents in this mutual venture, you're "buying in" to the "community." That buy-in makes it easier to work out problems the group may face, as well as individual problems your child may be having with another kid. As SportsMoms, we've seen how a foundation of parental cooperation operates to benefit a group and its players. One of us has also had a particularly nasty experience with a team that lacked that cohesion.

One of our sons was on a local soccer team that we were with from the beginning. There was a real sense of camaraderie and mutual support among the parents. After a few years, a number of new kids in the area joined the team *en masse;* however, despite our friendly overtures, their parents made it clear in word and deed that they were not about to take the time to form a working relationship with the rest of us. Soon afterward we faced a crisis over Coach's behavior.

Remember earlier when we related a story about a coach who verbally hounded a child because he was shorter than average? That was *this* coach. One day, things came to a head when Coach's cruel and unceasing harassment sent this resilient, likable kid home in tears, and he refused to come back. We "old" parents recognized that Coach had stepped way over the line, and that the time had come to take a stand. We could not be silent and allow our children to think we condoned Coach's behavior. So we tried talking to Coach, but he didn't give an inch. We next went to the club officials, but even with their urging, he refused to apologize. When we appealed for support from the "new" parents, their reaction was *If you don't like it, why don't you just leave?* They were in the majority by then, so we couldn't force the issue without their support. We ended up doing what they suggested: when the season's commitment was up, we left.

Leaving wasn't sour grapes on our part: we felt it was the only alternative. If we'd stayed, our presence might have led our children to believe it was okay to be cruel to someone. We also had to let our kids know that sometimes it's necessary to take a stand, despite the price you pay for doing so. But leaving was a shame, because it changed what had been an otherwise-fabulous situation for our athlete. Even sadder, it didn't have to turn out that way: over the years, we've seen more serious problems than this one resolved by SportsParents willing to cooperate.

You can foster camaraderie in ways big and small. Invite the team and parents to your house for pizza. Agree to take part in transportation caravans to away games. Spend time around the pool together when you stay at a hotel during tournament time. Take another SportsMom's kid to practice when she has a scheduling conflict. Show up on a chill Saturday morning with a large thermos of coffee and lots of extra cups. (Cookies will earn you bonus points.)

Don't dominate team meetings with your particular concerns. Don't gossip about other parents. Don't criticize their kids' play or their sidelines' behavior, no matter how much you want to scream, "Can't you get that %$#@* kid to behave?" Always give your Fellow SportsMom the benefit of the doubt.

In the process of building these relationships, you'll also learn how much you can rely on each parent. Do you trust SportsMom A to drive your kids to practice? If SportsMom B says she'll take responsibility for your child at an away game, what does she mean by that, and can you count on her to do it? If you're in charge of the team fund-raiser, can you rely on SportsMom C to complete her committee assignments on time?

Fund Raising

Speaking of fund raising…well, we must, because it's a Sports Fact of Life. It is also another way in which parents form that foundation of cooperation we've been talking about.

SportsMoms who have already paid playing fees are often surprised to discover that they're expected to do their part to raise money for uniforms, a special event, travel, or a sports camp. Some teams also raise funds to help cover the fees of

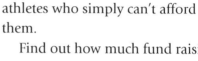

athletes who simply can't afford them.

Find out how much fund raising your child's team requires *before* you sign on. Some people will tell you that if you don't want to give you that if you don't want to give your time, you can just write a check, but we've found that's not always wise. First, you're missing out on a prime opportunity to build a relationship with the other parents. Second, unless it's a *very* big check, your lack of willingness to pitch in and do the dirty work will be duly noted and held in the collective memory bank for a long, long time.

If you're involved in organizing a team fund raiser, consider the following:

- What is the purpose of this fund raiser and what is your goal? Be explicit: new uniforms; a trip to an out-of-town championship; scholarships for deserving players. How much money do you need to raise?

- Do you have a plan? Can the other parents and Coach live with it? How will you involve the athletes? (We consider this a must: otherwise, the Lesson of Life they learn is that someone else should do the work so they can play.)
- What contributions of time and money do you expect from team parents? Do you provide options for those parents who can afford only time or money, or more of one than the other?
- How will you generate community/business support? How will you recognize and show appreciation for it?
- Is your timing right, or are you competing with other major fund raisers in your community? Do you have a back-up plan if your event is dependent on good weather? Will the fund raiser be safe? Consider such issues as the safety of selling items door-to-door, or if you need insurance coverage for a car wash.

If you're in a position of influence in this fund raiser, don't lose your perspective. It's important to let other parents find their own comfort zone. Some will put more into it than others. On the other hand, a so-so fund-raising parent may turn out to be a terrific carpool-to-practices parent, so don't worry too much about things being absolutely equal in this particular endeavor.

When the fund raiser receives community support, return the favor in the form of community service: organize your team to clean up a park or trash along the highway (check with local government for ideas and permission). Do not, however, make more work than necessary for parents. If the kids can't handle themselves in a supervised but independent fashion, do not make the offer.

In planning a fund raiser, keep in mind that you're limited only by your imagination and what the market will bear. Here are some ideas that might work in your child's sport:

- Bring in a college or professional athlete as a speaker.
- Sell something: clothing, sports paraphernalia, fruit, candy, holiday baskets.
- Have athletes do yard work (supervised, of course) for a donation.
- Wrap holiday packages at a local mall.
- Hold a car wash.
- Have parents and supporters contribute items to an auction or garage sale.
- Organize a food-and-fun get-together for families (spaghetti supper, pancake breakfast).
- If your athletes are in their mid to late teens, hold a one-day sports clinic/camp for younger athletes.

The Case for Good Manners

Despite all we've said about building a working relationship with other parents, you're not always going to get along with everyone all the time. Some of your Fellow SportsMoms (or Dads) may drive you up the wall. What do you do then?

Be polite.

It's that simple. You need not be best buddies or always agree, but you should be civil. Not only should you do this because it is right, but also because it is smart. By being polite, you are serving as an excellent role model for your child.

We think there needs to be a renewed emphasis on politeness in our society, and, being SportsMoms, we see no reason

SportsMom™

"Little Katie's mommy sure has a great left hook..."

why it should not begin on the playing field where it's known as *good sportsmanship*.

Aren't we all a little tired of seeing professional athletes who don't get their way throw their rackets, get in the ref's face, or berate Coach? Do you suppose that this began when they became adults? With all due respect to their SportsMoms, we'd venture to guess it started earlier, the very first time they weren't required to be civil when things didn't go their way.

Hold your child to a higher standard than that. Teach him that he may disagree with a decision, be disappointed with a game, or even fighting mad at an opponent who taunted him, but none of these things is an excuse for bad manners. He can blurt out his feelings to you in private later, but you expect him to maintain a certain standard of conduct on the playing field—and off, for that matter.

Help your child identify situations that provoke him, then devise strategies for handling them. Ask him to think about the rude kids he knows: what do other people think of them? Make him realize that his good reputation is all he really has in life, and that every time he's rude, he throws a little bit of it away.

Coach should be your ally in this endeavor. It's reasonable for you to expect him to be in control of himself, and set the tone for civil behavior during practice, in the dugout during a competition, or at the motel where you're all staying at tournament time. Coach should not scream at the kids or the ref, or erupt in uncontrolled anger, no matter how frustrated. It's also fair to expect Coach to control the kids: no spitting at the competition or trash-talking, no crossing the line of what is considered acceptable behavior in that sport.

However, then we get to the issue of other parents. What most SportsMoms want is for Coach to handle those parents who yell obnoxiously or belligerently at refs, kids on either team, or even Coach himself. In these cases, what we'd like Coach to do…well, what we would really like is best left unsaid. What we expect is that Coach will deal with these parents privately and quietly, reminding them of what behavior is expected, and what will not be tolerated.

That's a reasonable expectation, but remember that, unless your team has rules on expelling parents who act like jerks, there is only so much Coach can do. This is where  you can support him. Start subtly: if, game after game, no one will stand next to an obnoxious parent, or if no one will carpool with him, he just might get the message.

However, given that subtlety rarely works, you've got another option. If you think his behavior is a real detriment to the team, and other parents share your viewpoint, go as a group to Coach and let him know you plan to talk to JerkParent. Then do it: be polite, but firm. He may not change, but at least you tried. You also have the option of simply ignoring the guy—completely. Whatever you do, do not lower yourself to his standards: tempting as it may be to subject him to the verbal barbs of your rapier-sharp wit, don't do it. You'll end up looking like a jerk, too.

Give the Ref a Break

Speaking of good manners, we highly recommend you employ them when it comes to referees, umpires, judges, and assistant referees, those hardy individuals who ensure safe and fair play by enforcing the rules of the game. Too often players and parents hurl inappropriate comments at officials, even show their total lack of respect with creative hand gestures.

In our book (the one you're reading), abuse of officials is unacceptable. Unfortunately, it's on the rise.

Abuse has caused more than one seasoned official to quit, as well as legions of teen refs who were recruited to learn the game and join their ranks. These folks barely get paid enough to stand in rain-soaked fields or on sun-parched courts, let alone become targets for the verbal darts of frustrated parents.

Are you guilty of this behavior? If so, we strongly suggest you consider what your example is teaching your child. (Excuse us while we climb onto our soapbox.)

First, you're teaching him that it's okay to not respect authority. That can come right back to slap you in the face because *you* represent authority, too. Second, you're teaching him that when things don't go his way, he can take out his frustrations on others without regarding their feelings. Finally, you're teaching him to devalue the knowledge of those who have spent much more time than he studying the game. All in all, not an ideal lesson plan for instilling character in your child.

You should also consider that you are humiliating your player when you—dare we say it?—act like an obnoxious bonehead. Being an embarrassment to your child is not a good foundation on which to further build your relationship.

Officials are trained for their positions, and the higher you go in your child's sport, the more trained they are. Give them the respect that knowledge deserves. And remember, just like the rest of us humans, they make mistakes. Yes, sometime a judge's or ref's mistake may cost your child a victory. But you know what? Stuff like that happens in life, too, so it presents a perfect opportunity for another Important Lesson of Life.

SportsMom™

© 1998 KBL

"Do you think maybe we're at the wrong field?"

Chapter 11

Keeping Your Head above Water

THERE COMES A POINT in every SportsMom's life when she asks herself the question *How am I ever going to manage all this?*

It's a good question. And if we could give you a surefire answer to it, we could move to a remote mountaintop, then wait for the SportsMom World to beat a path to our door.

However, even though we don't have a surefire answer, we do have a lot of suggestions that can help you better manage the SportsMom experience.

Realize That Something's Got To Go—And It Need Not Be Your Sanity

Were Mr. Spock—that bastion of logic on *Star Trek*—to look at the circumstances you're in now, he'd have no trouble explaining why you're having problems handling it:

> There are only 24 hours in a day, Captain SportsMom. My analysis shows that, as a typical mother, you spend an average of six sleeping, another eight working, and approximately 2.5 on meal preparation and consumption. Preparing for work and your commute takes two hours. You spend an average of 2.5 hours a day devoted to household tasks, and another 0.5 hours running errands. An additional hour is spent helping your children with their homework. Prior to your offspring's involvement in youth sports, the remaining 1.5 hours were devoted to a variety of miscellaneous but necessary tasks, as well as occasional brief periods of relaxation and conversations with your partner.
>
> Given these facts, I can come to but one conclusion: it was illogical to think that you could add another time-consuming obligation to your schedule when you were already booked 24 hours a day. To put it in Earth terms, Captain SportsMom, it is only logical that something has to go.

Make it so, SportsMom.

Look at your schedule and figure out what you must eliminate, curtail, disregard, or delegate. Does your home have to be *House Beautiful* perfect all the time? Must meals be elaborate affairs? Is there a high school kid who'd be willing to run errands in exchange for a few bucks? Are your kids doing their fair share of household tasks?

Decide what's important to you, set your priorities, then make the changes necessary to fit the youth sports experience into your life. However, there is one change we strongly recommend against: do not try to pick up more time by shorting yourself on sleep any more than you already have. (You're *supposed* to get eight hours, you know.) You may gain a few hours if you do, but they'll be offset by the fact that you're not operating at peak efficiency and alertness the rest of the day.

Although Mr. Spock's analysis assumed that SportsMom worked outside the home, our advice also goes for stay-at-home mothers. Your schedule may be different, but it is undoubtedly just as full, so you, too, will have to make adjustments to accommodate this commitment to your child's sport.

Manage Your Time

Even if you've established priorities and made adjustments, you still need good time management skills to make things go smoothly.

Some SportsMoms are seemingly born knowing how to plan their time. Then there are the rest of us who could use some pointers, so here goes:

- Use a calendar or day planner, and keep it with you at all times. We're amazed at how many SportsMoms don't. Instead, they keep everything in their heads; however, as remarkable as most SportsMom heads are, there's a chance you're going to forget something when the pressure's on.

- Keep phone numbers in your planner/calendar, including the car phone numbers of your nearest and dearest.
- If your budget can handle it, invest in a cellular phone.
- Keep a file for each of your children's activities (notices, etc.), then enter the date and location in your planner/calendar.
- At the beginning of each week, work out the details of the next seven days. Figure out where you'll be going, what your priorities are, and what supports need to be in place to make certain all the pieces come together.

Advance planning makes every day easier, but it's essential to get you through those times when life hits critical mass. It helps you handle a half-dozen schedules that require everyone to be in a different place at precisely the same time, not even counting the dinner party and parent-teacher conference. Here are additional ideas for those crazed days when you're really strapped for time:

- Keep a phone book in your vehicle so you can order a take-out meal to be picked up on the way home.
- Ask for help. Can another parent pick up or drop off your child? Make it clear that you'll return the favor.
- Talk to your kids before you get to practice, the game, or whatever. Make certain they understand you're on a tight schedule, so there's absolutely no talk time after they're done with their activity.

In addition to preserving SportsMom Sanity, planning has an added benefit. Your child will see, firsthand, how it's done, then apply the approach to homework, play practice, and other activities. There is nothing like "do as I do" to get the lesson across.

Don't Obsess

Although we've been talking about the importance of planning and time management, we don't want you to think that all will be lost if every item on every list for every day isn't checked off in perfect order.

Don't get blown out of the water if things go wrong or if you're unable to perform each item on your list perfectly. There are lots of times in life when "good enough" is fine. If you don't learn to roll with the punches, you'll end up frustrated, short-tempered, brittle, or even depressed. Even worse, you'll be teaching your child to do the same when events don't go as planned.

It's not always easy to be flexible and adjust on a moment's notice, or to lower your once-high standards, but you must learn to do these things for your sake and your child's. Take a deep breath and ask yourself, "What's the worst thing that could happen as a result of this situation?" Unless your answer is *Someone might die*, it's not that serious, SportsMom.

These are lessons we've had to learn ourselves, so we know it's possible. In fact, one of us—the one who, by nature, is inclined to set impossibly high standards for herself—once faced a situation where she had to make a compromise that would have driven her straight up the wall years earlier:

> *My five- and seven-year-old boys had to attend a pretournament soccer practice. They were also scheduled to perform at a piano recital. There was enough time*

between the two events to make it to both, but not enough time to clean up and change clothes. So, in the midst of all the little girls in their lovely dresses and boys in handsome blue blazers, my two sons took their place at the piano with grimy faces and soccer uniforms, leaving clumps of cleat-shaped mud in their wake. Their Coach wasn't happy because they left practice a tad early, and their music teacher disapproved of their attire. But it worked for my children and me!

We think the lesson to be learned from that story is that the interests of your kids should always come first. You may have to table your high standards and your pride to do it, or stop worrying about what others will think, but it's worth the sacrifice.

If You're Flying Solo

Much of the information we've covered in this book is relevant no matter your marital status. However, we want to spend a few moments on the special challenges facing single SportsMoms. And that's quite a few of you: in 1998, twenty-three percent of all the kids in this country were living in mother-only households.

We think the biggest advantage the Single SportsMom has is that's she's not under the illusion that a partner will help shoulder the load. As the single member of our team puts it, "At least I knew up front that I had to handle this myself. The married SportsMoms usually don't come to that conclusion till halfway through the first season."

Don't get us wrong: we are not bashing men. We like men. We respect men. We have good relationships with men. But face it: with rare exceptions, aren't women usually the ones who end up initiating and managing the family schedule? Isn't it SportsMom who organizes the team banquet and washes uniforms and makes the appointment for the pre-sports physical? Doesn't the entire family count on her to remember who needs to be where at what time?

However, we also recognize that while most of the responsibility usually falls to SportsMom, a married SportsMom does have the advantage of having another responsible adult handy whom she can recruit in a pinch, or count on for at least some regular contribution to the cause.

Single SportsMom doesn't have that backup, unless her child's other parent lives in the same town and has committed to being involved in his child's life, including his sport. Even then, it's wise to plan as though you are flying solo, just in case something arises in his life that prevents his involvement.

If you are a Single SportsMom, you must be big on plans, because you can't always do everything yourself. You need a plan if you have multiple children who need to be different places at the same time. You need a backup plan in case you're sick and can't drag yourself out of bed to drive your child to a tournament. You need a plan in case a work obligation prevents you from getting your child to practice on time.

Planning requires you to ask others for help. If you pride yourself on being self-sufficient, suck it up and park your pride at the door for your kid's sake. Enlist the help of relatives and friends. Find a nice SportsMom on your child's team and ask if she could help out when you have a conflict. Above all—

think ahead. The night before the team leaves for a weekend competition is no time to be tracking down a ride for your child.

Besides scheduling, the other major challenge you may face as a Single SportsMom is that your child's father may not be involved in his life.

This means that your child—boy or girl—doesn't have a dad to serve as a guide to the traditionally-male bastion that is sports. In the future, when more SportsMoms themselves will be former athletes, the sports hierarchy will probably

SportsMom™

"Thanks for taking Jimmy home with you. I'll be there soon."

change. In the meantime, it's essential that you find a male relative or family friend who can help your child navigate and understand this traditionally "guy" thing.

If your child's dad isn't around, you'll also have to deal with a situation that will occur over and over—and is guaranteed to rip your heart out every single time. That is, when the competition is over and all the other kids are exchanging high-fives with their dads, or when talk turns to the post-game play-by-play analysis, there's going to be a huge hole in your child's life. Don't ignore his pain or attempt to minimize it. Tell him you know it hurts. Let him know you hurt with him. Then fill that hole in his life the best you can.

Sports present opportunities to help you do that. While there's no way that another adult male can replace what a father can provide his child in terms of emotional support and guidance, the right male coach can be a good role model. Sports give your child the chance to form relationships with other children and their parents. Finally, sports provide you and your child the opportunity to grow even closer as you share experiences and spend time together. Again, none of these things can fully substitute for a father, but they can help fill the gap.

Chapter 12

Keep Your Eye on the Goal

IF YOU'VE MADE IT TO THIS POINT in the book, you no doubt recognize the tremendous role the youth sports experience can play in helping your child grow, develop, and learn Important Lessons of Life.

Youth sports—at any level—provide a means to shape your child's character, his values, and his relationship with you, your family, and others. Sports can build his self-confidence, show him how to work with others, and help him deal with authority. They can teach him how to handle victory and defeat, and how to respect and relate to those who have more talent than he does and those who have less.

Sports can instill good fitness habits at an early age, and may even keep your child out of trouble.

Because sports require you and your child to spend a lot of time together, you have the opportunity to grow closer, and to maintain that closeness at a time when many other youngsters pull away from their parents. That time together means that you learn more about your child, and he learns more about you. He has the chance to see how you act in a variety of situations, then follow your example. And, because all this connecting takes place in an arena your child chose to be in, he's more willing to participate.

But none of these good things that can result from sports just happen, SportsMom. That's where you come into the picture. Your job is to interpret and frame your child's sports experience so he learns those Lessons of Life, so that he grows and develops the way you want him to.

Never lose sight of this role. Sure, you've also got to handle the day-to-day details, like getting nutritious food on the table and delivering your child to practice. You have to work with Coach and the other SportsMoms and juggle a thousand other demands that never quit. But don't become so wrapped up in the everyday folderol of the sports experience that you lose sight of the big picture. Always remember the chief responsibility of using the sports experience falls to you.

As we've said throughout this book, this is not always an easy job. It requires wisdom, inner strength, tenacity, patience, a sense of humor, and a lot of other positive qualities that most SportsMoms possess in abundance.

You *can* do this. There's no one better qualified for the job, because there's no one in the world who loves your child more or knows him better. So trust your instincts. Use your head. And never lose sight of your goal: to use the sports experience to raise a happy, healthy, decent human being.

Good luck and godspeed!

Selected Bibliography

Child Growth and Development

Bell, Ruth. *Changing Bodies, Changing Lives.* US: Random House Times Book, 1998.

Hughes, James B. *Synopsis of Pediatrics, Fifth Edition.* St. Louis, Missouri: CV Mosby Co., 1980.

Gruber, Howard E. and Vaneche, J. Jacques, eds. *The Essential Piaget, An Interpretative Reference and Guide.* Northvale, New Jersey: Jason Aronson, 1995.

Poinsett, Alex. "The Role of Sports in Youth Development." Report of a Meeting convened by the Carnegie Corporation of New York: March 18, 1996. (http://www.carnegie.org/reports/point1.htm)

President's Council on Physical Fitness and Sports. "Physical Activity and Sport in the Lives of Girls: Physical and Mental Health Dimensions from an Interdisciplinary Approach." Council Report: Spring 1997. (http://www.kls.coled.umn.edu/crgws/pcpfs.html)

Pruit, David B., MD, Ed. *Your Adolescent's Emotional, Behavioral and Cognitive Development from Early Adolescence through the Teen Years.* (American Academy of Child and Adolescent Psychiatry) New York: Harper Collins, 1999.

Parenting

Bylsma, Dan and Jay. *So Your Child Wants to Play in the NHL.* Chelsea, Michigan: Sleeping Bear Press, 1998.

DeFrancis, Beth. *The Parent's Resource Almanac.* Holbrook, Massachusetts: Bob Adams Inc., 1994.

Jordon, Deloris with Gregg Lewis. *Family First: Winning the Parenting Game.* New York: HarperCollins, 1996.

Kindlon, Don, and Thompson, Michael. *Raising Cain: Protecting the Emotional Life of Boys.* US: A Ballantine Book, 1999.

Rosemond, John. *Parent Power! A Common Sense Approach to Parenting in the 90s and Beyond.* Kansas City, Missouri: Andrews and McCeel, 1990.

Schafer, C. *How to Influence Children.* New York: Von Nostrand Reinhold, 1982.

http://rtpnet.org/~jacobs/essays/e_kids.html. "Kids Sports: Your Dreams or Theirs?"

Injury

Renstrom, P.A., Ed., *Clinical Practice of Sports Injury Prevention and Care, Second Edition.* Boston: Blackwell Science Inc., 1993.

http://www.goodhealth.com/gh_mag/marapr97/youngath.html. "How to Train Young Athletes."

http://web.boston.com/globe/sports/packages/youth_sports/part3.htm. "Larry Tye: Injured at an Early Age."

http://www.kidsource.com/kidsource/content/news/baseball.3.11.html. "Ten Health Tips Every Youth Baseball Coach Should Know." Issued by Temple University Hospital.

http://jan.ucc.nau.edu/~kkt/EXS300/Skeletal.html. "The Skeletal System and Its Articulations."

http://www.uconnhealth.org/diseasewellness/disease/HealthTopics/Orthopaedic%20.../young.ht. "The Young Athlete."

Training

Douillard, John. *Body, Mind and Sport: The Mind-Body Guide to Lifelong Fitness and Your Personal Best.* New York: Harmony Books, 1994.

King, Douglas S., et.al. "Effect of Oral Androstenedione on Serum Testosterone and Adaptions to Resistance Training in Young Men." *Journal of the American Medical Association,* June 2, 1999, pp. 2020-2028.

White, Timothy, and the editors of the University of California at Berkeley "Wellness Letter." *The Wellness Guide to Lifelong Fitness.* New York: Rebus, distributed by Random House, 1983.

http://www.goodhealth.com/gh_mag/marapr97/kidssports.html

Nutrition

Berning, Jacqueline R. "Healthy Eating Tips." Splash: Official Magazine of USA Swimming, Volume 7, Issue 1, February 1999, pp. 12-13.

D'Hooghe, Michel. *Soccer and Nutrition.* Federation Internationale De Football Association, 1994.

Kirschmann, Gayla J. (as contributor) and John D. *Nutrition Almanac, Fourth Edition.* New York: McGraw-Hill, 1996.

http://thriveonline.aol.com/kids/sports.nutrition.html. Clark, Nancy. "Ready, Set, Grow." March 22, 1999.

http://www.sportsparents.com/medical/index.html. Noden, Merrell. "Eating Disorders and Athletes."

Other References

The journals and websites listed here were either reviewed by the authors for general information/background, or cited within other references used.

Journals

Journal of Pediatric Healthcare

Science, Technology, and Human Values

Journal of Marriage and Family

Websites *(these tend to change)*

http://www.anatomy.gla.ac.uk/fab/public/docs/growth2.html

http://www.gbod.org/youth/articles/howlearn.html

http://www.gulftel.com/~scubadoc/agediv.html

http://www.justwomen.com/archive_experts/experts14.html

http://www.deetya.gov.au/schools/publication/genderequity/6_2.htm

http://www.seattletimes.com/extra/browse/html97/altmath_073197

http://hammock.ifas.ufl.edu/txt/fairs/59709

http://www.texnews.com/1998/texsports/pregno0515.html

http://www.allkids.org/Epstein/Articles.html

http://web.utk.edu/~mwoodsid/overhead1.html

http://www.ma.psu.edu/~nmh2/ch2ohs.htm

http://www.use-gymnastics.org/publications/technique/1996/6/tasks.html

Index

P.S.

If you have any topics or issues you'd like to explore further, any questions for SportsMom, or would simply like to give us your feedback, we can communicate via **www.sportsmom.com.**

At this website you'll find our column, *SportsMom Suggests*™, which deals with one issue at a time (more specifics on health and nutrition, how to handle a car full of rowdy athletes, when your child is the new kid on the team, etc.), the SportsMom Grapevine™ (links and resources you may find useful), SportsMom™ comics, an *Ask SportsMom* feature (sort of an electronic  Dear Abby® for SportsMoms), and, of course, an opportunity to buy our books and other stuff.

You can also e-mail us (hello@sportsmom.com); snail-mail still works well, too (SportsMom, P.O. Box 993, Maumee, OH 43537). Just know that we'd love to hear from our Fellow SportsMoms: we can all use all the support we can get.

- 183 -